OBVIC

OBVIOUS

CHOICES

Can I Really Believe?

By Mike VanBruggen

Published by:

www.GroundedFaithPublications.com

Copyright: 2015 Mike Van Bruggen
All Rights Reserved

Obvious Choices

Dedication

I would like to dedicate this book to my family, Fran, my wife of 25 years (and counting) who has loved me and supported my dreams and accomplishments every step of the way, our children, Ethan, Bret, and Rachel, who are all young adults now and endeavoring to serve the Lord however He may lead, and my parents, John and Betty, who sought to impart the Wisdom of God's Word to me from my beginning. I would also like to acknowledge the impact the Word of God has had on my life, through it HE has brought me to Salvation and Security in His Son, Jesus Christ.

My Hope

What I hope to explain in this book was not obvious to me as a child but became obvious as the Lord's faithful stewards explained real truth to me. Please allow me to be one of those faithful stewards in your life as you read this book.

My Life So Far

Born in 1959 in a small city in Michigan, I grew up in a 'church home' with loving parents. After trusting Christ for salvation at an early age I wandered from the faith during my teens. Thankfully the Lord did not wander from me and in my mid-twenties I restored my relationship with HIM. Fran and I were married in 1990 when I was thirty. After working in various factory jobs, at the age of 46, Fran and I felt the calling of the Lord on our lives, I quit the factory job and enrolled in the Word of Life Bible Institute and subsequently became Missionaries with Word of Life to the country of South Africa.

Table of Contents

Prologue – pg 6   Under-Informed

Chapter 1 – pg 8   The Choices We Make

Chapter 2 – pg 17   The Amazing Bible

Chapter 3 – pg 49   Get Out of the Fog

Chapter 4 – pg 63   Is He Able?

Chapter 5 - pg 84   Need More Light

Chapter 6 – pg 108   It's Obvious Who "I AM"

Chapter 7 – pg 124   Why is Jesus the Only Savior?

Chapter 8 – pg 140   Take it!

Epilogue – pg 152   What Happens Now?

Prologue

Under-Informed

I believe that in the events of human relationships the obvious needs to be stated. The reason that I believe we need to state the obvious is because the obvious may not be obvious to everyone. Then, by definition, it is obvious that the obvious is not always obvious. –Mike VanBruggen

We make many choices in life based on limited information. Many of these choices are not important and making the wrong choice won't really hurt us. Other things are very important and the wrong choice will definitely take us where we do not want to go. We can't decide what to believe because some important key facts are unknown to us. We want to hedge our bets and play both sides because we don't really know which is right. Once we have an adequate number of facts, the decision becomes much easier, if not obvious.

When it comes to the subject of God, I believe people are under-informed about the facts and over-informed about the fiction. We let everybody's personal view on the subject influence us. Some movie star or sports hero can tell us anything, and we'll believe them because they are famous. Facts are not glamorous and research is not fun. But at the end of the day, if we want to know the truth, we must do the work.

Getting more facts from more sources should help us with more confidence about God, knowing what He expects from us, and how we should respond to Him. I didn't write this book as an exhaustive study that nobody would read. Rather I wrote towards a few specific highlights that point to one thing that I think is obvious. That God is real and He wants us to have a relationship with Him. Once we are settled on that fact, the Obvious Choice is to get to know HIM!

Chapter One

The Choices We Make

We make choices every day. From the moment we wake up in the morning until the moment we fall asleep at night we make choices. Even when you think you don't have a choice you do. You might chose the option leading to the greatest pleasure, the least stinging consequences, the least expensive outcome, or the least path of resistance. Truly we cannot escape choices, they are facts of life.

There are many mundane choices we all make on a regular basis. When will I get up today? Shall I brush my teeth? Do I need a shower? Am I going to work? What do I want for Lunch? Do I want a salad with dinner? These are only a few of the hundreds of choices we make each day. We've got to decide. We've got to choose. If we say "I don't care," that amounts to a choice to let someone else decide for us, and a choice is made.

What about the whole group of occasional choices we make about needs that we don't even know exist, until someone points them out. Things like, "Would you care to donate to this cause today?" "Would you like a FREE estimate on some new windows for your house? Those tired old windows are costing you a fortune!" "Do you want the warranty with this purchase, for a small fee? You won't need to pay for any repairs!"

These choices are not so obvious; we need to make a decision based on an unknown factor. Would my donation help this cause? Are those new windows going to save me enough money to pay for them? What is the likelihood this retail item will break under normal use? Once I asked the sales person "is this item going to break, because if it is going to break I don't want the purchase". The salesman said 'this is a quality product...no one ever brings these back for repairs...you'll get good service out of this unit'...yak, yak, yak! So I'm like, "Well, I don't need the warranty, thanks for pointing this unit's reliability out!" Whether I get the warranty or not is not going to greatly impact my life. This is a choice to either pay more for this product or less.

We all have big choices in life, the things that will impact our quality of life or maybe even the length of life. I remember when I was a young adult, (I remember because my mother has never let me forget), an empty lot in a good neighborhood was coming up for sale within walking distance of my parents' house. Now being about twenty years old I had my mind set on a new pickup truck. The truck was big, black, and beautiful! Monster trucks had started to come to the forefront as attractions at the county fairs. Not really a 'monster truck' but a street legal version of one with a lift kit, big tires, chromed wheels, four wheel drive, roll bar, a huge V-8 engine with plenty of power, and an incredible sound system, the truck was amazing! I had a decent job and had the money to get either the shiny new truck that I could drive around and show off in, or the empty lot in a good neighborhood which I would have to mow and pay taxes on.

Obviously my parents thought it would be good for me to buy the lot; we would be in the deal before the Realtor would get involved making this a better deal, valuable real estate! Obviously my twenty year old mindset was more focused on the truck and you can guess which I purchased, yes I bought the truck! My parents thought they made the complete argument for the undeveloped lot and that obviously I would choose my only best option and buy the lot, but I did not. Mom realized too late what I had done and she asked me why I bought the truck and not the lot? I still remember this event and the feelings involved thirty years later. I answered and said to mom, "I can't drive a "lot"". I thought I had a fantastic point but my reasoning made no sense to her at all. I wish I had a buck for every time I've heard that line quoted back to me, I'd be rich today!

I had great times with my truck. Man, I drove the truck everywhere! I drove on road and off road, all over the mid-west. I drove the truck to Disney World! I drove the truck over sandy beaches to launch boats and up and down sand dunes for fun. I drove the truck to move friends, haul appliances and I drove to help the Police deliver food to old people during a major snow storm!

This is my favorite truck story; I drove the truck back into an open field during the same snow storm and pulled out three snowmobiles stuck in the snow! That truck had the POWER! Nothing stopped that truck except a gas station! (And I think the truck stopped at every station we saw!) My truck got 13 miles to the gallon, loaded, unloaded, uphill, downhill, pulling a trailer or not, in the snow or not, consistently going 13 miles on every gallon of gas. At the time this was not a big deal because gas was 65 cents a gallon and the expense was worth it to me because the truck was so cool! She was such a fantastic truck and always looked good...until rust began to show. About that time gasoline surged to about $1.25 a gallon which became a big deal! In fact they were talking about rationing gas which was going to be devastating for me! Finally, I parted company with my old friend the truck. Every time the gas price went up the trade value of my truck went down. I had trouble finding a dealer who would even take my truck as a trade in.

Meanwhile, our neighbors bought the property which they still own to this day. They planted a couple of trees and kept mowing the lot all these years. The neighborhood is situated near a medium sized lake in a medium sized city. The lake is good for all water-sports, swimming, fishing, sailing, skiing, boating, and in the winter the ice freezes hard. We played hockey and ice skated on the lake as children and snowmobiles were always on the lake zinging around. We even had people with pontoon air planes landing on our lake. Just a few years after I didn't buy the property, a neighborhood association formed. They purchased the rights and land at the lake and developed a 'neighborhood private park'. As the Association incorporated and developed the lake property all the land values went up significantly, including the lot that I didn't purchase at a discount price. Now thirty some years later the lot is worth about twenty times the amount I could have bought it for originally.

Today the truck is long gone and there is only one Polaroid to prove the truck's existence! Now obvious to me, my parents had greater insight than I and I should have bought the property and not the truck. In life all choices are not obvious to us immediately, hindsight offers us a new perspective but we cannot go back and choose again, the deal is done. I couldn't recognize the value in the property and I wouldn't listen to the advice of those who did, and I paid the price. The investment I made in the truck just drifted away until I got almost no value returned to me when I traded the truck in. The property not only held its value but multiplied its value time and time again! Because of what I now know, I would make a different choice. Obviously the better choice would be to buy the property!

We make choices based on who we think we are, what we think we would like to do, where we think we want to be someday, and how we think we might get to that location in life. I thought as a young adult I could handle everything. I thought I would rather drive a cool truck than mow a dirty old lot. I thought only about today and never considered 'someday' would come. I called my 'someday' next week and I thought I would arrive in a cool truck. Now as a middle aged adult I wonder if I'm grown up yet, and even though I have more knowledge than I did thirty years ago, I can't even imagine how many things I don't understand.

My greatest satisfaction is now found in helping others realize their ultimate dream. My 'someday' is called eternity and I understand how I'm going to get there, because of what I understand about God and the Bible, the choice is obvious!

The obvious choice is apparently not always obvious. What seems obvious to me now was not obvious to me thirty years ago. If only I had known at age twenty what I know now. Perhaps the sight of a rusty pickup truck thirty years in the future compared to the value of the real estate thirty years in the future would cause me understand the obvious choice was to buy the lot. I didn't investigate the options with the future in mind, I was focused on the here and now, and I lost future benefits due to the choice I made.

When we come to the 'choice' of God I believe the choice is obvious, but I know it is not so apparent to everyone. The problem is most people don't sit down and take a good hard look at the subject. Most people are trying to fit in, trying not to cause turbulence, trying to appease family and friends so as not to disturb anyone. This approach works fine for the here and now (everybody stays within their parameters and everything is good) or so we think.

Inside us is a churning, a longing to find the truth, a sense that there is more to life than these few years we have on earth. We feel we need to make a choice yet not knowing what the choice is. The choice is about God.

A nice thing would be if we could wait until the end of a matter before we make our choices, everybody would win every time! Starting as toddlers, waiting to see which of our friends has the most fun, then decide who we would play with. As children on the playground it would be nice to find out who is going to win the game before we decide which side we are on. Finally, waiting to see which High School will have the best football team, the greatest marching band, or the teachers with the least homework! The choices would be obvious based on what we want, what we hope for, and what we need.

In the choices in life are not so obvious to most people. People bring many different philosophies to choose from and they are obviously different from each other, but which is right? Would we choose the pickup truck or the valuable real-estate? Would we choose for the here and now or would we choose what is best for us in the long run?

I believe there is an obvious best choice and the choice is open to all. In the same way that I needed to understand the long term implications of my choice between the Pick-up truck and the valuable real estate, people today need to understand the difference their choices will make in the next thirty, one hundred, even one million years!

In a million years (or a hundred years for that matter) it won't matter much who won the championship last year or who we disagree with next year. If God is real, (and He is) what will matter years from now will be what our understanding of and obedience to God was in this life. If God is not real, nothing really matters beyond today.

My prayer is that we will together be able to see clearly those things which should be obvious. The Bible is what it says it is; that Jesus is who He says He is, and that He did what He said He did. Once we've settled those issues the choice should be obvious what to believe about Jesus. (He died for you and me and more! He was buried and rose again in victory over death and He overcame our sinfulness to take us to Heaven to be with Him. It will be obvious that we can trust God, and better yet, know Him.)

Chapter Two

The Amazing Bible

General information about the Bible

Communication of any kind is an intriguing kind of thing. To think that someone from another part of the world can sit down at a keyboard and write a letter to a friend or relative and at a touch of a button that letter can be transported instantly around the world to the recipient! With a few keystrokes a response can be quickly returned! Even better, the same message can be sent and received from a cell phone! You can send a text message from your seat on a bus in Kalamazoo, Michigan to your friend who might be in a taxi in Johannesburg, South Africa! To me this ability is mind boggling, unbelievable, and to be honest, incomprehensible! Yet I believe it can be done, in fact I know these things happen every hour of every day that we live.

Even though I know these amazing and incredible communications work, I have no idea how they do it. Even if it were explained to me in detail I'm sure I wouldn't understand how it works, but I believe it does! I've seen the evidence of text messages first hand, I've sent and received e-mail personally, I 'instant message' my children in New York while I'm at my mission post in South Africa. I believe it without fully understanding it.

The communication God sent us is called the Bible. I have heard it referred to as 'a text message from God' and 'God's love letter to mankind'. I've also heard the Bible described as irrelevant and outdated although I don't believe that this observation is correct. The Bible is the most amazing, improbable, and important book ever written. Please let me share a few things about the Bible that you might have never thought about.

First let's talk about some of the basics of the Bible. The Bible is an ancient book, or actually a book of sixty-six books. It is a library of books written within a time frame of about 1500 years beginning around 1450BC and finishing in the first century AD. There are more or less forty different authors of the sixty-six books within the Bible. These authors were from various regions and backgrounds writing in three different languages. What we now call the Old Testament was mostly written in Hebrew with a few passages written in Aramaic. (Some of Ezra and Daniel, along with one verse in Jeremiah, are written in Aramaic.) The New Testament was written in Greek. Greek was the scholarly language during that time in Earth's history.

Just think about that for a minute. In our culture today you can't find 40 authors who agree about anything! Try finding 40 from the last 1500 years who agree even in different languages from different places! The sixty six books of the Bible complement each other in every respect.

Furthermore, these books are not revised; they are as they were when they were originally written. We have more manuscripts, and older manuscripts of the sixty six books than we have of any other ancient manuscript. These ancient manuscripts, some dating back to the 2nd century BC, when compared to the current manuscripts prove the reliability of the text.

With respect to the Old Testament the oldest copies are those found in the caves near Qumran, dated back to about 150BC and the Biblical Scrolls there prove the incredible accuracy of our current texts. The Old Testament manuscripts are unchanged from our oldest copies. About the New Testament Author and Scholar Charles Ryrie reports; "More than 5,000 manuscripts of the New Testament exist today, which makes the New Testament the best-attested document in all ancient writings".[1] The texts of both the Old and New Testaments are not revised or changed in their content. They are reliable, standing the test of time.

Being scrutinized over the centuries the sixty six books are today recognized as what's called Canon of Scripture. This can be understood as the "standard" of Scripture. The Scripture of the Old Testament was recognized as meeting the standard of scripture early on; certainly by the time of Jesus the 39 books of the Old Testament were recognized and used as scripture. The test of authority was that the book had to have been written by a prophet, lawgiver, or leader in Israel. The New Testament had to have the backing of one of the Apostles. For example, Mark wrote in conjunction with the ministry of Peter. Luke and Acts were written by Luke who was under the authority of the Apostle Paul. Beyond that there had to be internal evidence that there was something different, something Godly, about the book along with the acceptance by the church fathers, those who studied the scriptures regularly.

There were probably thousands of other things written during those times but none of those meet the 'Standard of Scripture'. They might be accurate historical accounts but they are not God's inspired word. By 397AD it is generally agreed that the Canon of Scripture was complete. The Sixty Six books that combine together to give us our modern Bible have not changed.

The Bible itself says in...

> 2 Peter 1:21 For the prophecy came not in old time by the will of man: but holy men of God spake as they were moved by the Holy Ghost.

Here we find the answer to how forty authors from different regions speaking different languages can write sixty six books that coincide and complement each other perfectly! There is really one author, God Himself through the ministry of the Holy Spirit!

Because God inspired men to pen the Scriptures, we can gain knowledge through them that pertain to life! To our lives!

> 2 Timothy 3:16 All scripture is given by inspiration of God, and is profitable for doctrine, for reproof, for correction, for instruction in righteousness:

The Bible is reliable and we can trust it to instruct us in what we should do, what we shouldn't do, how to fix what we've done, and how to keep on course. It proves to be a valuable asset to anyone who will accept and follow it. After about 3500 years it is still relevant to the modern person because it deals with the principle things in life. Other ancient writings are old and outdated but the principles God has set forth work everywhere and in every situation that they are faithfully applied. It is alive just a God Himself is alive!

> Hebrews 4:12 For the word of God is quick (alive), and powerful, and sharper than any twoedged sword, piercing even to the dividing asunder of soul and spirit, and of the joints and marrow, and is a discerner of the thoughts and intents of the heart.

The Bible has the unique ability to work within our soul as it is a standard bearer that can discern our innermost deeds, the thoughts and intents of our heart. No other book has ever claimed the ability to do that. The principles can be applied to every situation each one of us can face with every expectation that they will work.

Prophetically Accurate

No other book in the world contains the number of prophecies nor the number of already fulfilled prophecies, none! Let's just consider the approximately 700 prophecies that pertain to Jesus. The odds that all 700 prophecies would or could be fulfilled in one man are incalculable; don't forget that these 700 prophecies were recorded by multiple human authors in different regions of the world in different generations. These factors further multiply the odds. Some of these prophecies were recorded thousands of years before Jesus was born and placed in that manger in

Bethlehem! What are the odds that any one man could fulfill all these prophesies from hundreds or thousands of years before?

These prophesies of Jesus included the place where He was to be born. The circumstances surrounding Jesus birth included that he was to be born of a virgin. These are not broad based all-inclusive prophesies, they are very precise, very specific, and very detailed. For example, no one could fulfill the prophesy of Jesus today simply because the timing is wrong.

In his book, Science Speaks, Author Peter Stoner partially answers this question. [2]Just consider 48 of the major prophesies concerning Jesus would produce odds of about 1 in 10 to the power of 157. That is 10 multiplied by itself 157 times. That is a BIG number! It is basically impossible for anyone outside the power of God to fulfill just 48 of the total prophetic statements about Jesus, yet Jesus didn't stop at 48. He fulfilled all of them except the prophecies that are yet to be fulfilled.

Mathematics and statistics conclude that Jesus' fulfillment of Bible prophesy was statistically impossible without the work of God behind it. Add to that the improbability of every other prophecy in the Bible coming true the statistics skyrocket. It is statistically impossible for the Bible to exist without God's inspiration and power. The odds would be incalculable, or 1 in $10^{infinite}$, you can't define it's such a big number. Yet God has done it, the Bible is really here, it's prophesies are really true, we can trust God's word statistically.

Genetics and the Bible

All of us carry the record of history in our bodies, it's in our DNA! We are each a unique edition of human history. We not only make history by our very existence, but by carrying the fingerprint of all the generations of our particular ancestors. As seen on TV, modern day technology can tell from a saliva sample who is the daddy and the mommy. (Why people watch some of these shows I'll never know... Worse yet, why would anybody voluntarily go on one of them?)

The same can be done for generations in history! All of us are just copies of copies of copies of people, people we call our ancestors. Nameless, faceless people who lived and died as our predecessors probably not even thinking about who we would be or what we would be like. Most of us just know two or three generations of our ancestors, yet we carry a record of them in our bodies, in our DNA. We can trace what part of the world our family came from, we can even tell if somewhere back in time one of our ancestors came in from another part of the globe! If your 5x Great Grandpa was from Europe and your 5x Great Grandma came from Asia, your DNA has a record of it! It seems intensely complicated and profoundly simple at the same time.

Since the genetic record and the science behind it is repeatable, testable, and observable then we can trust it, it is actually science. Therefore when we follow the genetic evidence we can draw concise and accurate conclusions from it! If the DNA evidence leads us to draw a specific conclusion we can trust it.

Where does the genetic evidence lead us? What does it say? Secular scientists were surprised where the genetic trail led them. Quoting Dr. Robert Carter... [3]"It comes as a surprise to most people to hear that there is abundant evidence that the entire human race came from two people just a few thousand years ago (Adam and Eve), that there was a serious population crash (bottleneck) in the recent past (at the time of the Flood), and that there was a single dispersal of people across the world after that (the Tower of Babel). It surprises them even more to learn that much of this evidence comes from evolutionary scientists."

Keep in mind the results evolutionary scientists would have wanted to find in our DNA. They would have loved to see much more variation in the gene pool, which would suggest that different kinds of humans could have "sprung up" from many animal sources around the planet. They would have expected to find that, for example, African individuals were vastly different from Asians who would be vastly different from Europeans. It is not so! The entire human population is genetically 99.8% identical! The Human gene pool itself does not fit the evolutionary theory; the Biblical account of creation does fit nicely.

The amazing Bible tells us where mankind came from...

> Genesis 2:7 And the LORD God formed man of the dust of the ground, and breathed into his nostrils the breath of life; and man became a living soul.

> Genesis 2:21-22 And the LORD God caused a deep sleep to fall upon Adam, and he slept: and he took one of his ribs, and closed up the flesh instead thereof; 22 And the rib, which the LORD God had taken from man, made he a woman, and brought her unto the man.

God made man and woman; just one of each. From there they reproduced after their own kind just as the animals were to reproduce after their own kind, (He made them too!).

While we are on the topic, remember the geneticists determined from the genetic record that there was a 'Population Crash'. The Bible records that too! There was a worldwide flood in the days of Noah and the entirety of mankind was lost except for Noah and his wife and Noah's three sons and their wives. Who knows how many people died in that worldwide catastrophe, but we know how many survived, just eight. The world was repopulated through only three of those four couples; there is strong evidence that Noah and his wife didn't have more children after that. Here is what the Bible says about it...

> Genesis 7:7 And Noah went in, and his sons, and his wife, and his sons' wives with him, into the ark, because of the waters of the flood.

> Genesis 9:18-19 NKJV 18 Now the sons of Noah who went out of the ark were Shem, Ham, and Japheth. And Ham was the father of Canaan. 19 These three were the sons of Noah, and from these the whole earth was populated.

The population crash, from millions of people to eight. The whole world repopulated from there!

Geneticists back this story up today, sometimes unwillingly, through tracing the "Y" chromosome and mitochondrial DNA. Noah came through the flood with his three sons, meaning as Noah passed his "Y" chromosome to his three sons because they are copies of Noah himself. Geneticists agree there is just one strain of "Y" chromosome in the world today. Evolutionist would be happy to find many strains of "Y" chromosomes, but there is just one. Scientists trace females through something called mitochondrial DNA; there were three wives for Noah's three sons. Do you want to guess how many strains of mitochondrial DNA there are in the world today? Yes, there are three! As a side note, science says that two of these strains are very close to each other while the third is somewhat different yet still of the same kind. This is how detailed the genetic record is that lives within us. Possibly, out of the three wives of Noah's sons two were sisters or close cousins. Pretty crazy isn't it!

How did we get where we are today with seemingly different people in different parts of the world if we all came from one source? The Bible has an answer for that too! After the flood of Noah mankind settled in one region and the population grew over many generations. God wanted mankind to spread out and subdue the earth but mankind stayed in a relatively concentrated area. They all spoke one language, and they all had the same customs. It was a homogeneous culture. God came and confused their languages so they would have to spread out.

> Genesis 11:7-8a Go to, let us go down, and there confound their language, that they may not understand one another's speech. So the LORD scattered them abroad from thence upon the face of all the earth:

How were the people scattered? Along their family lines according to the sons of Noah!

> Genesis 10:32 These are the families of the sons of Noah, after their generations, in their nations: and by these were the nations divided in the earth after the flood.

The Geneticists have mapped out where they think the different people groups migrated, backing up the Biblical record. Our genetics are telling us our history!

Our eyes are different, our skin is different, our hair is not the same, so how can we be the same? These are legitimate questions; let's think about this for a few minutes. Scientist do agree there is only one race of people, we are all one kind. Any person from any part of the world can breed with any person of the opposite sex from any other part of the world and make an offspring. We cannot successfully breed with any other species, and if we were different in kind (See Genesis chapter one.) from each other we would not be able to breed across kinds. Still, being of one kind we can readily see that there are physical differences between us, in fact we are individually unique!

What we commonly call 'people of different races' are really 'people of different groups'. The book "One Blood" states [4] "The truth is that these so-called 'racial characteristics' are only minor variations among the people groups. Scientists have found that if one were to take any two people from anywhere in the world, the basic genetic differences between these two people would typically be around 0.2 percent but these so-called 'racial' characteristics that many think are major differences (skin color, eye shape, etc.) account for only 6 percent of this 0.2 percent variation, which amounts to a mere 0.012 percent difference genetically."

The things we think make us different are just family characteristics and minor mutations that have accentuated themselves over time. Our different cultures and language barriers are the differences we notice. The scientific evidence supports what the Bible says, the people of the world are not different but the same!

> Acts 17:26 And hath made <u>of one blood all nations of men</u> for to dwell on all the face of the earth, and hath determined the times

before appointed, and the bounds of their habitation;

Genetics, the history that is written in our DNA, syncs so comprehensively with the Biblical accounts of Creation, the Great Flood, and the Dispersion of the post flood community at the Tower of Babel, that it cannot be a coincidence.

Astronomy Science and the Bible

Have you ever looked up into the sky and ask yourself 'I wonder how that works', I have! I grew up during the great space race in the 60's, I would stay up at night to watch NASA's live feeds to the networks. Blast off! I loved all the coverage. I was amazed at the equipment. I thought the astronauts were more important than the president or the greatest sports heroes. I mean these guys were landing on the MOON! To this day every time I see a Hubble Space Telescope photo of something in space I stop and check it out. I love it, but I don't have the big equipment to stargaze. I just let scientists and astronomers show me what they find.

Over hundreds of years in man's history here on Earth we have found out there things about the universe that we _thought_ we knew but were seriously mistaken. There must still be things we don't know about the cosmos, but what we do know has changed dramatically over our history. Aristotle, who lived between 300 and 400BC, thought the Earth was the center of the universe and that everything revolves around us. Most people would think of Aristotle as extremely smart but none of us believe we are the center of the Universe.

When I grew up all the text books said that people who lived around five hundred years ago believed the Earth was a flat round disk. You can search the internet and find that some ancient societies described the Earth as round but apparently not everybody came to the same conclusion, or information was lost during history leading later civilizations to conclude that you could fall off the edge if you sailed too far.

This all sounds silly to us, we have pictures from space that clearly show the Earth from several different angles, the world is round, actually it is a sphere. We understand that we can go straight west and eventually return to the same spot where we started. Just as an ant can travel around a baseball we can travel around the globe of the Earth. The first circumnavigation of the Earth was by the expedition of Ferdinand Magellan, 1519 – 1522AD. Although Magellan did not complete the trip himself that expedition did prove that you could go west to get to the east.

Roughly 2200 years before Magellan's expedition Isaiah wrote...

> Isaiah 40:22a It is he that sitteth upon the circle of the earth,

We believe what Isaiah recorded. The Earth is round, and it's big. Compared to other planets it might not be that big but compared to humans this world is HUGE! It is estimated that the Earth [5]weighs 5.97×10^{24} Kilograms or 13.16×10^{24} pounds! The Earth's circumference at the Equator is 40,075km or in other words it is 24,901 miles[5]. It is easily the biggest, heaviest thing we have ever touched! Ever think about that? Where do you put something that big?

There is the old riddle that goes something like this, "When you invite a 2000 pound Grizzly Bear over for dinner, where does he sit? Answer, anywhere he wants!" So the Earth can be wherever it wants because it is so big, right? No...it wouldn't work that way! The Earth is exactly where God intends for it to be and nowhere else. The relation of the Earth to the Moon, the Earth to the Solar System, the Solar System to the Galaxy, and the Galaxy to the entire Universe is all a delicate balance created by God.

Back to the question of where do you put a planet? What supports it? How does it stay there? Another quick internet search will reveal that ancient Hindus believed the earth to be supported on the backs of four elephants, which stand on the shell of a gigantic tortoise floating on the surface of the world's waters. The Earth of the ancient Vedic priests (somehow associated with Hinduism) was set on twelve solid pillars; its upper side was its only habitable side, (flat Earth). The Altaic people of Northern Siberia affirm that three great fish support the earth. The Tartars and many of the other tribes of Eurasia believed the earth to be supported by a great bull. Which do you think is right?

There is one more; Ancient believers in the God of Heaven believed God hung the Earth on NOTHING! Whew! That is hard to imagine, how could that happen? This Earth weighs in at some amount over 13×10^{24} pounds and has a circumference of almost 25,000 miles, how could you hang it anywhere? Think of an ordinary Christmas ornament, they might be about the same circumference as a baseball but not as heavy. The Christmas ornament will hang on a branch but the baseball would pull the branch down. Now the Earth would require a really big branch or beam to hang on, but God hung it on nothing!

We were talking about pictures from outer space showing the Earth to be round; did you ever see anything there supporting the Earth? Are there any elephants or fish? What about a bull or pillars? I don't see it hanging from a rope. (How big would that rope have to be?) There is nothing there. The Earth is suspended in space. To oversimplify it, the force of gravity to the Sun is countered by the centrifugal force of the Earth's orbit. We are hanging on NOTHING just like the Bible says!

> Job 26:7 He stretcheth out the north over the empty place, and hangeth the earth upon nothing.

So really, is it easier to believe that God set up the orbits of the planets and offset those orbits with gravity to keep everything going in a predictable way, or that there is a giant fish holding things in place? Science continues to back up what the Bible says!

Continuing in astronomy, did you know that the Universe is still expanding? Until fairly recent history we didn't know from a scientific standpoint what the universe was doing. Here is an excerpt from an article I came across recently. [6]*For thousands of years, astronomers wrestled with basic questions about the size and age of the universe. Does the universe go on forever, or does it have an edge somewhere? Has it always existed, or did it come to being at some time in the past? In 1929, Edwin Hubble, an astronomer at Cal-tech, made a critical discovery ... he discovered that the universe is expanding.*

What Edwin Hubble discovered in 1929 the Prophet Isaiah wrote in about 700BC, about 2600 years before science caught up to God. Here is the passage for you.

> Isaiah 40:22 It is he that sitteth upon the circle of the earth, and the inhabitants thereof are as grasshoppers; that stretcheth out the heavens as a curtain, and spreadeth them out as a tent to dwell in:

God spread out the universe (Heavens) and continues to spread them, He has made the universe as a place, (tent), to dwell in. He hung the Earth, the place habitable by humans, on nothing inside a tent we call the universe so we can have a place to live. He continues to stretch the tent and keeps everything in balance so we can continue to inhabit the Earth. Pretty nice!

I don't want to talk a lot about evolution or evolutionism but at this point I just have to say that the expanding Universe could make the Big Bang theory look pretty good. Think about this, we can take any one thing and develop a theory that works based on a limited set of circumstances. I can sell you a car, a real sporty model. It is candy apple red with a spoiler and really big tires on the back, just like a dragster! It looks great! I can tell you the car won 100 races and now I've made it so it gets great gas mileage. You might be interested? But then you walk to the other side of the car and find the door is badly dented and the window looks like it is rolled down but you find no glass in the door. It looks awful. You open the hood and find there is no motor so it doesn't use any gas anymore and it is not going to win any races anytime soon. When I told you a limited amount of information about the car you were interested (admit it☺), but when you found additional information your interest dropped dramatically. When you look at things, big things like expanding universes and hanging planets on nothing you're going to have to decide what you believe is most plausible, most possible, what fits best when you get all the additional information.

This leads us to another question. How long has man inhabited the planet Earth? Some scientists will tell you that we've been here millions or billions of years. These are the same scientists who want to believe mankind came from several sources, and that we are different from each other (we've already discussed some of that). Other scientists say that mankind has been here on the Earth about

6000 years give or take. These scientists find the evidence that exists to support the young earth theory rather than the millions or billions of years that some say. Let's investigate a few things and try to get a glimpse of the entire thing like we did with the car.

There are hundreds of things we know as facts but we don't apply them as evidence toward scientifically deciding what we believe. We were talking about me growing up watching the NASA Moon shots. Oh, how I loved the adventure and mystery! I'll just pick a couple of interesting things concerning the Moon to illustrate why I believe in the young earth.

First, did you know the Moon is moving away from the Earth? It is about an inch and a half further away than it was on this date last year. It is interesting and factual. It has to do with the tides in the oceans, the Moon causes the tidal motion and the tidal motions pull forward on the Moon accelerating it ever so slightly. The rate is measureable and predictable, with some certainty we can say how far away we expect the Moon to be in one hundred or one thousand years. We can also say where it was in the past.

Most of us would hear a statistic like that and say so what? Well here is what...we are just a mathematical equation from determining where the moon was six thousand years ago, or six billion years ago and try to draw a conclusion about what that means.

About 6000 years ago the moon would have been about eight hundred feet closer to Earth than it is now[7]. Eight hundred feet isn't enough to make a big difference to either celestial body, things would have been essentially the same. You can basically say that the relationship between the Moon and Earth would be the same over a six thousand year period. Even if you expanded the time frame to ten thousand years the differences would be negligible.

In the scope of six billion years you cannot really calculate the distance because if you rewind the Moon's orbit just 1.4 billion years the Moon would collide with the Earth[7], let alone six billion or billions and billions. It just doesn't work. Billions and billions just does not work.

Secondly about the Moon, there is no atmosphere! Unlike the Earth which is protected by the air or atmosphere that we live in, the Moon has nothing but space around it. Outer space is not totally empty like I was taught in school, there is dust in space. I don't want to get overly complicated about dust but it is known and scientifically accepted that a certain amount of dust falls on the Moon every day, every month, every year. This certain amount of dust is also scientifically accepted to fall at a certain rate; it falls on the Earth too! On the Earth the atmosphere incinerates some of it and what comes through is picked up in the wind and blown about, we could never have an opportunity to collect it and measure it. On the Moon there is no wind because there is no atmosphere so the dust would fall evenly and accumulate over time.

Have you ever seen a picture of the Lunar Module that NASA used to land on the Moon? It had big round pads on each foot, and the legs were much taller than they needed to be. The round pads were big enough for Neil Armstrong to stand on before he stepped onto the Moon, so they weren't little. When you're talking about blasting something into space you're really concerned about weight above most anything else. Why would NASA put big round pads and extra-long legs on the Lunar Module if they were not needed? Because they didn't know how much space dust they were going to find on the Moon's surface.

If the young Earth theory was right there would be just a couple of inches of space dust on the Moon. If the old earth billions and billions of years theory was right there might be several feet of space dust there. What did those Astronauts, Neil Armstrong and Buzz Aldrin find when they arrived? There were just a couple of inches of space dust, not several feet.

Here is a transcript of Neil Armstrong talking from the surface of the Moon...'*I am at the foot of the ladder. The LM* (lunar module) *footpads are only depressed in the surface about one or two inches, although the surface appears to be very, very fine grained, as you get close to it. It is almost like a powder. Now and then it is very fine. I am going to step off the LM now.* (Then the famous first words from the surface of the Moon.)*That is one small step for man, one giant leap for mankind.*' (Parenthesis mine)[7]

There are many more of these very practical items to look at that all point back to the fact that the Earth is young. Not coincidentally the Bible has genealogies and dates so we can reconstruct a timeline history of the generations from creation until now. The generations add up to roughly six thousand years. Remember all we have already said and (I hope you're going to finish the book) add in all that you're going to read, you can see how the science of astronomy support the Bible.

Archeology Supports the Bible

To be honest Archeology doesn't really excite me too much. While there are tons of archeologically significant finds that concern the Bible and even the test of the Bible I'm afraid if I stay here too long you'll get bored and leave. Still I want to touch on the subject and say there has never been an archeological find that has disproved anything in the Bible. There have been countless finds that support Biblical places, Biblical events, and the textual reliability of the Bible. The field is so big that there are many books and web sites to which one can refer. However, I don't want to completely ignore archeology.

You would not have to be a Biblical scholar to have heard of King David. Even if you only know the story of David and Goliath you've heard him, it's the same guy! David's dad's name was Jesse. David was the youngest son of Jesse, he watched the family's herd of sheep. David went to visit his brothers at the battle and got himself into his battle with Goliath, ultimately defeating the Giant with a sling and a stone. David was anointed the next King of Israel and when the time was right David became King of Israel. King David was arguably the greatest King Israel ever had. David is a major figure in the history of Israel and in the narrative of the Bible.

King David was widely talked about in scripture and in legend but there was no physical evidence that the famous King or of Israel as a nation until 1993. While excavating an ancient mound called Tel Dan in northern Israel archeologist discovered a chunk of basalt with words carved into it. The translation was "House of David" and "King of Israel"[8]. Rock solid proof that there was a King David and there was a Nation of Israel. Remember, in archeology absence of proof is not proof of absence[8]. There are innumerable archeological discoveries that support the Bible and no discoveries that disprove it.

The Bible is Historically Accurate!

History is a very tricky thing; different people see things in different ways and with a different emphasis. There doesn't necessarily have to be a 'right' and a 'wrong'. Depending on where the reporter is situated it might limit the experience for them while another reporter situated in another location could have a more complete story.

When I was eleven years old my dad took me to the Major League Baseball All Star Game, it was 1971 and the game was played in Tiger Stadium in Detroit. It was a huge thrill for me, at that young age I was already a huge baseball fan! I could have told you the major stats of every Detroit Tiger and I knew all about most of the players that would be in the All Star game. Believe me, I was on every pitch.

In that game a young outfielder named Reggie Jackson homered, hitting the ball off the light tower in deep right center field. I mean it was very far away from home plate and probably a hundred feet up in the air! An eleven year old little leaguer could only dream of hitting a ball that far. The tickets we had for that game were out in left field, we were back up under the upper deck so we could not see anything up in the air. I remember seeing Reggie hit that ball, I instantly knew it was a homer, wow that ball got out of there fast! I didn't know that it hit the light tower until we got back to the Hotel and we saw the highlights! I went crazy, half excited and half disappointed because I hadn't seen it, but I was there! I did see the ball land back on the field; it didn't go into the stands. Years later I was talking to someone that was there that day too. We were comparing stories about that home run. From his seat he saw the ball hit the light tower then he went nuts about it, but he didn't see the ball come back on the field. I couldn't see the tower but the outfield grass was right in front of me and I couldn't miss the fact that it didn't stay in the stands.

Both of us have seen the film clip of that home run, both our history was right but because of where we were in the stadium our histories were different,

OBVIOUS CHOICES — MIKE VAN BRUGGEN

not wrong, but different. The major facts were accurate in both cases and the TV camera caught the whole thing.

The Bible is an accurate and reliable history book, and it is corroborated by outside historians. By 'outside historians' I mean historians who are not writing under the inspiration of the Holy Spirit. (Secular historians)

Just like the TV account of the All Star game was corroborated by something like 55,000 baseball fans that were at the game that day. There are countless accounts in other society's histories outside of Israel that back up the Biblical accounts. For example there are reports of a worldwide flood in almost every culture in nearly every part of the world! These legends and oral histories serve as additional witnesses to Great flood of Noah.

It is true that secular history supports the Bible. I want to focus on a couple of accounts concerning the crucifixion of Jesus and the persecution of those who followed Jesus. In the writing The Antiquities of the Jews, Bible times historian Flavius Josephus writes: *"Now, there was about this time Jesus, a wise man, if it be lawful to call him a man, for he was a doer of wonderful works—a teacher of such men as receives the truth with pleasure. He drew over to him both many of the Jews, and many of the Gentiles. He was [the] Christ; and when Pilate, at*

45

the suggestion of the principal men amongst us, had condemned him to the cross, those that loved him at the first did not forsake him, for he appeared to them alive again the third day, as the divine prophets had foretold these and ten thousand other wonderful things concerning him; and the tribe of Christians, so named from him, are not extinct at this day."[9]

Another early historian, <u>Cornelius Tacitus</u> in the writing The Annals: *"Consequently, to get rid of the report, Nero fastened the guilt and inflicted the most exquisite tortures on a class hated for their abominations, called Christians by the populace. Christus, (Jesus Christ) from whom the name had its origin, suffered the extreme penalty during the reign of Tiberius at the hands of one of our procurators, Pontius Pilatus, ..."*[9]

When there are corroborating accounts of historic events from outside sources it validates the reported events. The point is that secular history does mention Jesus, does mention His Crucifixion and that He rose again on the third day! It was obvious to them that something amazing was going on whether they could understand it or not.

A Summary Statement

Truly an entire book could be written within each category I briefly discussed here, even so we can obviously see that the Bible is accurate and reliable to us today. Since we can obviously conclude the Bible is accurate and that the only explanation of its very existence has to be the very presence of God in its writing, then we can conclude that we should give it the respect that it deserves. When we decide to respect the Bible is the Holy Inspired Word of God, His written revelation to mankind, we should take heed to it. In order to take heed to the Bible, we must know what it says, and then we need to apply it to our lives. It is really just that simple!

[1] Charles Ryrie; Ryrie Study Bible, How we got our Bible, Is our text reliable, 3rd paragraph.

[2] Peter Stoner, Science Speaks, Chapter 3, The Christ of Prophecy.

[3] Adam, Eve and Noah vs Modern Genetics by Dr. Robert W. Carter http://creation.com

[4] *One Blood, The biblical answer to racism by Ken Ham, Dr Don Batten and Dr Carl Wieland* Chapter 3 Genetics and the human family.

[5] Wikianswers.com

[6]

http://skyserver.sdss.org/dr1/en/astro/universe/universe.asp

[7] Answersingenesis.com

[8] agards-bible-timeline.com

[9] http://www.clarifyingchristianity.com/b_proof.shtml

Chapter Three

Get Out of the Fog

My wife, Fran, occasionally tells a story stemming from her childhood about her family going on a road trip. Mother, Father and four children packed up in a station wagon (remember those?) with a trailer full of a family sized tent and camping supplies. The trip was to the western United States from Michigan, they kind of drove to the northwest seeing Mt Rushmore, passed through the Badlands in South Dakota. They ventured through the Rocky Mountains to Oregon to visit family. Staying on the move they made their way south to the Grand Canyon (a highlight of the trip for sure) and then they made their way back to Michigan from a southwest route seeing beautiful Colorado along the way. It was an ambitious schedule for the family; they only had about two weeks' vacation time!

With the schedule being so tight, driving, camping, and visiting National Parks there was not much room for adjustments to the schedule. The day they were going to be at the Grand Canyon, the canyon was fogged in. They couldn't see across or down, it was just fog. The family tried to make the best of it, visiting the gift shop, having a picnic lunch, the children running and playing on the grounds, waiting for the fog to lift. Finally the family had to leave the Grand Canyon without even seeing one rock face or cliff even though they were right there. To this day Fran has never seen the Grand Canyon, she has been there but not seen it.

Some years later when the family was grown Fran's Parents went back to see what they could not see before. This time there was no fog and the canyon could be viewed in all its natural beauty.

Mom and Dad were reflecting on the first time they were there with the kids and fog, they remembered the gift shop, where they parked in the lot, where they ate lunch, and where the kids ran and played all those years ago. From where they ate their lunch the view would have been spectacular without the fog and where the kids played was so close to the edge that it scared them! The kids played RIGHT THERE when they were little, just steps away from a several hundred foot drop off! Fran's mom said later that the kids wouldn't be playing there if she could have seen through the fog. Now that everything was in plain view it was a beautiful yet frightening sight!

The first time there, with the fog in place nobody was taking tours of the canyon, you couldn't see anything. The next time with the fog out of the way and the canyon spread out there before them, many people were touring the canyon, discovering the beauty, the enormous size, and the incomprehensibleness of the creation we call the Grand Canyon!

Sometimes when we talk about God and Heaven we feel kind of the same way, like we are in the fog. We cannot see clearly, we cannot understand how close or how big God is because it seems foggy to us. Fran's parents went back to the Grand Canyon to see and the fog was lifted. Sadly many people see the "fog" when it comes to God and never return to see if the 'fog' has lifted. When we talk about God being in the 'fog' it is not He who has hidden himself there. In fact, it is the opposite. God is not 'in the fog' where we cannot see in. We are 'in the fog' and cannot see out!

How can things that seem so obvious to some people be so clouded to others? The Gospel, the truth of what Jesus did for us, is obvious to those who have accepted Him, but not at all obvious to those who have not.

Now that we have established the Bible as a library of books, a book of supernatural origin, then we can look into the Bible and find the answers we need to make these Obvious Choices! It only makes common sense that the publication God provided us would have the direction we need to seek out and find the answers to the big questions in life; who am I, why am I here, what should I do?

To read the Bible and try to figure out what in the world it is talking about can leave some people feeling like they are in that fog at the Grand Canyon. I think this is a common experience among most people at one time of their life or another. I don't think I've ever met anybody who totally understood the Bible from the very first time they read from it. I can also say I know hundreds of Christians who have studied the Bible for years and yet find new applications from the Bible to put into their life. We just can't understand God completely; He is too big, to complex, and infinitely beyond human comprehension. We can understand some things about God, and more importantly, we can grow in our understanding and relationship with Him! We can come out of the fog, into the light, and see the wonders that He has placed before us!

God's Word, the Bible, is a book that can lead us out of the 'fog'. It can communicate God's truth to us no matter if the events of our life twist and turn or pitch and roll.

> 2 Timothy 3:16 All scripture is given by inspiration of God, and is profitable for doctrine, for reproof, for correction, for instruction in righteousness:

We all know what the word profitable means; we are going to gain from God's Word. Here we are going to gain in four areas; doctrine, reproof, correction, and instruction.

Doctrine is just another way of saying teaching. The Bible is profitable for our teaching about God. The more we learn about God, who He is and what He does. We begin to see through the fog and we can begin to relate to Him and know Him.

The profitability of reproof shows us what is wrong in our lives. Lots of people don't want to admit that there are things in their life that are wrong, they might even have a double standard that says what is right for them might not be right for anyone else. It is something called relativism; it is a black hole that our society has embraced, and we're stuck in it. Having said that, there is a way out...

Follow some simple reasoning with me.

> - If there is no way the Bible could exist without the supernatural intervention of God...

>> -Then we've embraced God's Word, the Bible, as true.

> - If God supernaturally inspired the Bible for us...

>> - Then God exists.

> - If God exists, and his Word is true...

- Then He made us because that is what the Bible says.

-If God made us...

-Then He sets the standards for right and wrong.

- If right and wrong are determined by God in His Word called the Bible...

-Then we need to find out what it says and follow it!

Just like that the 'fog of right and wrong' is gone, it is clear because right and wrong are measured according to God and it is the same for everybody.

Correction complements reproof. Once you find that something is wrong, you need to know how to make it right. Correction is very profitable in light of the reproof because the Bible does not just leave you hanging there. There is an avenue to restoration for all of us!

And finally the profitability of the Instruction in righteousness, or basically how to stay right after reproof and correction has taken place! This is really where you get into a close relationship with God Himself. He has said what is right and wrong and you're conforming to it!

If you let God's Word operate in your life to the extent that you are being taught by it, accepting it as the authority for right and wrong, using it to make corrections, and growing in your relationship with God through it...then the fog is gone and you can see God more clearly!

The Next Step!

I can sense already you're thinking, how can a book that is between 2000 and 3500 years old tell me what is right and wrong in this modern century? They didn't have cars and busses; there was no television or movies and peoples religious views have changed a lot since then. What would those people know about modern society anyway?

Actually the answer to that is surprisingly simple. Let's review for a minute. Remember we talked in chapter two about the forty authors of the sixty six books that make up the Bible and that God through His Holy Spirit influenced those writers? This was how we determined that the forty authors, from various geographic regions, over a time span of about 1500 years could write sixty six books that coincide and complement each other without contradiction or error.

The verse we used said...

> 2 Peter 1:21 For the prophecy came not in old time by the will of man: but holy men of God spake as they were moved by the Holy Ghost.

The writers, holy men of God, were "moved" by the Holy Spirit meaning that God Himself wrote the Bible through men! From the original language we get the picture that the translation "moved" is kind of like the moving of a ship under sail in a fierce wind, the ship is going to go where the wind is going! God, through the Holy Spirit, determined where the writer was going with his text; He supervised and would not allow an error or contradiction.

Now knowing that God Himself wrote the Bible through men, holy men who followed Him, we can say that God knew the future and found a way for the words written up to 3500 years ago to still be relevant to mankind today. Some things, the most basic things are just spelled out like...

> Exodus 20:15 Thou shalt not steal.

Simple and concise, nothing to think about, just don't steal. Other things are not so clear on the surface but as you grow in Bible knowledge you find the answers, and it is surprising how obvious some of those answers are.

The answers are found in the guiding principles of Scripture. Before I begin to explain this let me say I believe the Word of God has all the answers we need to live a successful and Godly life! The Bible is alive because it's guiding principles can make application to situations we face today that could never have been anticipated by any human author that lived two or three thousand years ago. It is alive because God is alive and He did know the situations we would be facing even before we were born! To me that is very exciting!

How would we figure out right from wrong if the Bible does not specifically address the issue in question? We know we should not steal because the Bible says exactly that, Thou shalt not steal! But what about using un-prescribed or illegal drugs for example?

Our society is trying to justify or legalize some of the 'lesser drugs' as being acceptable based on the lack of danger to the user and civilization.

Should we accept public acceptance as a green light toward using these 'lesser drugs'? Not so fast. We might race to this conclusion if we really want to justify this issue but what is right? Remember God says what's right and wrong. God's word does have something to say about this even though there is nothing specifically saying "Thou shalt not use these 'lesser drugs'.

In the Bible we find the clear principle of Authority. Authority is given and taken away by God, it is His to delegate as He sees fit.

> Daniel 2:21 And He (God) changeth the times and the seasons: He (God) removeth kings, and setteth up kings: He (God) giveth wisdom unto the wise, and knowledge to them that know understanding:

> Proverbs 8:15-16 By me (God) kings reign, and princes decree justice. By me (God) princes rule, and nobles, even all the judges of the earth.

God is the ultimate authority and the authority that He allows to rule under Him needs to be obeyed.

> Romans 13:1 Let every soul be subject unto the higher powers. For there is no power but of God: the powers that be are ordained (ordered) of God.

> 1 Peter 2:13-14 Submit yourselves to every ordinance of man for the Lord's sake: whether it be to the king, as supreme; Or unto governors, as unto them that are sent by Him for the punishment of evildoers, and for the praise of them that do well.

If it is against the law of man to use these 'lesser drugs' then the principle from God's word to obey authority would prohibit us from using them.

Now we can kick this to another level, what if we live in a place where man's law does not outlaw the use of these 'lesser drugs'? Can we go to that place and participate with those who are indulging in this activity? Let's keep digging into the Biblical principles and see what God's word says!

With a little bit of looking we can find the principle of taking care of your body and doing proper things with it.

> 1 Corinthians 3:16-17 Know ye not that ye are the temple of God, and that the Spirit of God dwelleth in you? If any man defile (destroy) the temple of God, him shall God destroy; for the temple of God is holy, which temple ye are.

The Holy Spirit of God dwells within you if you have trusted and accepted Jesus as your personal Savior. If you have not trusted Jesus the Holy Spirit is not within you but you still owe God your health because He made you. Not only that, but you were made in the image and likeness of Him!

> Genesis 1:27 So God created man in his own image, in the image of God created He him; male and female created He them.

Since we belong to God (because the creator owns his creation) whether we trust Him for our eternal salvation or not, we are to keep ourselves in good physical health. There are many medical problems associated with the 'lesser drugs' (depending on which you pick and what you call lesser) Some examples would be, smoking anything is directly associated with lung disease, compounds that enter your blood stream may alter the normal function of your blood, your bodies filtration system (liver, kidneys, lymph nodes) are put under undue stress effecting their longevity and so on. God's principles would guide us AWAY from using them based on health concerns.

So, you might be thinking, if I can find a place on earth where the drug is not illegal and I can find one that has no medical problems associated with it then I can go ahead and do as much of that as I want! Not so fast! There are more principles to factor into the equation. These things can become addictions and can modify your behavior, which is what drugs do. Where do we look? Back to God's word!

> Ephesians 5:18 And be not drunk with wine, wherein is excess; but be filled with the Spirit;

We should not be voluntarily under the influence of alcohol or any other drug, (or activity's like video

60

games or internet usage out of control) but we should be "filled with" or voluntarily under the influence of the Holy Spirit of God. God should be our operating system in this life that He gave us. When we give that operating system over to an influence other than God, no matter what it might be, we are in violation of a principle of God's word, we must avoid that activity.

You might be thinking, 'Well then, if I can just keep it under control then it will be alright.' Not necessarily, in the area of clean internet usage or video games you might be able to say that. We are allowed recreation and fun, no problem there! The problem comes in when an activity begins to control you, changes your behavior negatively, and dominates your time so that you're not doing the things you need to do to keep up at school or work. This is especially true when it hinders your relationship with God – and it always will.

In the area of drugs, even if we are talking about 'lesser drugs' and alcohol, you would have to determine when they are effecting your personality, when they are hurting your relationships with family and loved ones, and of course when they are hindering your walk with God.

Note: If you have been affected, would you (in your altered state) recognize that (or how much) you have been affected?

Here is a passage that will help us with many of the choices we need to make...

> Romans 14:21 It is good neither to eat flesh, nor to drink wine, nor any thing whereby thy brother stumbleth, or is offended, or is made weak.

This principle from God's Word really answers the mindset caused by our desire to 'work the system' and find a loophole to exploit. Anything we do that causes another brother (or sister) to sin is a sin to us as well.

Our relationship with God and the Bible is not a system whereby we can get HIM to sign off on our sin. Rather it is an opportunity for us to accurately determine what HE would like to see us do and say, then do and say it! God's principles can guide our lives. They determine right from wrong in every instance, and they are reliable! God's Word does not change! We need to trust what God has said and be willing to apply it honestly to our lives. We will be the benefactor of living a Godly life and our friends and family will benefit from our positive example, which is a Biblical principle as well!

Chapter Four

Is He Able?

We have seen how God in His great plan pulled the Bible together utilizing many different writers over a great number of years. We have seen that just the prophetic record of the Bible sets it apart. There is no other book of prophecy that can even come close to the perfect record of the Bible, none. We looked at the Bible from a historical and scientific standpoint to see that it holds true in every respect, and it seems as though God has been active in all of it!

Is God able influence His creation today? Has mankind grown beyond God's ability to intervene in its affairs? After all He's getting pretty old! Almost every time we see an artist rendition of God He an old gray haired guy who can't manage to shave anymore, and by the looks of that gray beard it has been some time since He got anywhere near a razor. Let's look at a few events and see if we can draw come conclusions about God and his abilities.

First, I want to look at a personal story from my own life. My wife and I have been working with the youth in our local church since before we were married. As an engaged couple we took on responsibilities with the elementary age youth, we thought we would have kids some day and wanted to experience children while serving our church and our Lord. We started with the school year and were married in the spring of the next year. We had almost one full school year of experience by the time we said our vows. We have been involved with teaching and discipleship of youth ever since!

Somewhere in there, maybe about the third year, I was burdened to do a pamphlet and tract drop in our neighborhood. We had just moved and there were kids riding bikes and hitting baseballs all over the neighborhood, yet I never saw any of those young faces in our Wednesday night youth program. God was just impressing on me the need to reach out to the youth of this new place where we were living. I was afraid, mostly of the parents, but also scared in general at the aspect of going door to door for the sake of the Gospel.

I must have set three or four deadlines for myself, each time I would conveniently find an excuse, another thing to do so I would not have time to canvas the neighborhood. Along the way the burden in my heart for those kids grew more and more intense. I was being torn between my conviction that those kids needed to know about the Lord and my fear of following through on that conviction. I was even losing sleep over it! Deep down inside I knew what the Lord wanted me to do, but would I do it?

After several failures to even start going out I'd had enough. I told Fran so I was on the record, 'this Friday when I come home from work I'm going around the neighborhood with tracts and literature for the youth group...period!" I had set the date and the time, this was the final time. The Lord allowed me a couple nights' sleep and I got ready. I would wear my little youth group uniform, I would go on my bike, the pamphlets were printed, the tracts were purchased, and nothing was going to stop me.

Now we lived in Michigan at the time and in Michigan you can get what we call "all day soakers', rain that settles into the area and won't leave for a couple of days. I watched the weather report on TV, there was a soaker coming and sure enough that Thursday afternoon it began to rain. It rained all afternoon and evening, just a steady rain going to mist and back to rain. It was still raining when I got up that famous Friday morning to go to work. As I would get little breaks at work I would check the weather and it did not let up, even into the afternoon!

I was determined to follow through on my promise to God and deliver that youth group material, rain or no rain I had to do this! I walked to my car in the parking lot at work in the rain. I drove home with the windshield wipers on the entire way, there was no let up. I parked in the garage and looked out at the rain before I went into the house. It seemed to be raining harder!

I dressed in the youth group uniform, put my printed material into plastic bags, and went for my bike. I didn't care how wet I would get, I was just trusting God to get me through! I pulled my bike out, got ready to go, and asked Fran to push the button that opened the garage door. The Garage door opened and it was still raining, I was telling Fran I would see her later, I was going through with it!

As I was about to ride out of the garage the rain stopped! Just like that the rain stopped! I didn't know how long the interlude would be so I took off right then. It was still overcast, the thick cloud cover that seems so natural in Michigan. I hurried through the neighborhood while taking enough time at each stop to answer all the questions of my neighbors. It took a couple of hours to visit every house on each of the streets.

As I finished at the last house I had a peace in my heart that I can't really describe, a peace that comes from knowing that I did what God wanted me to do. It was a peace that only God could give. I rode my bike back home just as dry as the moment I left my garage except for my feet which had been walking through wet grass and getting splashed from the puddles.

I remember what happened next like it was yesterday. I rode up my driveway and coasted into the garage and within ten seconds it began to rain again and it didn't quit for another day! The only explanation I can apply to that amazing couple of hours was God and His ability to manage the weather for His purposes. Since that day I know firsthand what I believed before, God is able!

God has ability beyond what we can imagine and beyond what we can even think; He is an incredibly amazing God! This God who I credit for holding off the rain so I could visit my neighborhood can do it because He brought it into being from nothing! The very first verse in our Bible says

Genesis 1:1 In the beginning God created the heaven and the earth.

God made it all! But do you know He did the work of creation in the most miraculous way possible! Genesis 1 tells us that God made the entire creation and arranged everything in just six days and to top it off he made it all out of nothing! There was nothing there when God spoke and matter came to be!

Hebrews 11:3 Through faith we understand that the worlds were framed by the word of

God, <u>so that things which are seen were not made of things which do appear.</u> (underline mine)

We can't really comprehend that! I mean, we can make a cake but we have to have the ingredients first. We can make a house, but we first have to have the materials. We can even travel through a city, but there first has to be a city there to make our way through. God made everything, but He did it without ingredients, without materials, and without anything to go by. That's incredible ability!

Remember we discovered the Bible to be a reliable resource in chapter two? We can begin to use it as evidence to discover the abilities and attributes of God so we can get a better understanding of Him! Remember, God is not far away and He wants us to seek Him and know Him. Let's look at some of the people in the Bible and how they experienced God's ability.

Moses saw God's ability firsthand.

The entire story of Moses is one of the most amazing stories that could ever be told, Moses' life is full of twists and turns, ups and downs, ins and outs. But out of the dozens of incredible events in Moses life probably the most defining event happened at the edge of the Red Sea. Moses had led Israel out of Egypt by God's hand and some wonderful miracles. Pharaoh reluctantly agreed to let Moses and the Israelites leave because God had made the Egyptian's lives miserable through the ten plagues. After Israel left Egypt Pharaoh had a change of heart and decided to chase Israel into the wilderness. God was leading Israel in a pillar of cloud during the day and in a pillar of fire at night. All Moses and the Israelites had to do was follow the pillar.

As they came to the banks of the Red Sea they obviously had to stop. People generally cannot walk on water. Pharaoh's army was closing in on them, and they were trapped at the water's edge. God was able to handle the situation. He knew where He was, and what He was going to do. God moved His pillar from in front of Israel to a position behind Israel therefore protecting them from Pharaohs army. Then God caused a strong east wind to come on the sea, and it divided the waters so Israel could walk across on dry ground!

Then, when all of Israel was safely on the other side, God let Pharaoh and his armies follow behind. I don't know what Pharaoh was thinking because a God who has the ability to divide the Red Sea would certainly have the ability to release the waters again, that would Just be common sense. At the sight of a small ocean parting I think I would stop and worship that God immediately, but not Pharaoh. His heart was hardened and he went forward into what would be a watery grave for him and his men.

Joshua saw God's ability firsthand.

The story of Israel about forty years later finds Joshua leading the nation. They are about to enter the Promised Land but they had to cross the mighty Jordan River. The Jordan River is way too big to just wade across, Israel had all kinds of things with them so even swimming across was not do-able. Was God going to be able to get them across? Joshua got His instructions from God, and they carried them out in faith!

The instruction was that as soon as the feet of the priests who were carrying the Ark of the Covenant hit the water, the waters would be cut off and the coming waters would stand in a heap beside them. In other words the waters of the Jordan would simply pile up deeper and deeper on the upstream side! The downstream side would empty out! Israel would cross on dry ground as they did in the Red Sea!

Now for me this seems even more fantastic than the Red Sea Crossing. The waters of the Jordan didn't stop coming, imagine how many gallons of water pass by any given point of the Jordan River per minute. The Bible says the waters piled up in a heap! It does not say it flooded the area upstream or anything like that but the water stayed within its banks and piled up there! God even has the ability to make His material world, in this case the water, obey Him even to overcome the laws of nature and gravity! He is able to control it all! It is out of my ability to fully comprehend, but God did it!

Elijah thought God was able!

Elijah the prophet and the wicked and powerful King Ahab of Israel had a little meeting. King Ahab tried to accuse Elijah of hurting the country. Elijah countered with the truth from God that it was the King and his very wicked wife Jezebel who were hurting the country. Elijah called for a test of the gods, a contest between the false god of King Ahab who was called Baal, and the living God of Elijah who was the God of his ancestors Abraham, Isaac, and Jacob. Elijah had the King bring the 450 prophets of Baal, and they invited 400 more prophets who worshipped the image that was said to be Baal's wife. Of course King Ahab would be there, probably some servants would be there to attend to the King. Elijah would face them in the power of the Lord but alone on Mount Carmel!

Here was the test; each side would fully prepare a sacrifice to *their* god but without fire. They would then call upon their god to send fire from above and accept the sacrifice. The God who could do such a thing would be God and the other would be disgraced. As the Bible reads it seems that the 450 prophets of Baal came, the King was certainly there, and Elijah was there. At minimum Baal's side had 451 people, the Lord God of Heaven had just one representative. Judging from those numbers we can be pretty sure that Elijah was confident in God's ability to deliver!

The Bible can be the most entertaining reading you'll ever see, check out this passage!

> 1 Kings 18:17-40 And it came to pass, when Ahab saw Elijah, that Ahab said unto him, Art thou he that troubleth Israel? 18 And he answered, I have not troubled Israel; but thou, and thy father's house, in that ye have forsaken the commandments of the LORD, and thou hast followed Baalim. 19 Now therefore send, and gather to me all Israel unto mount Carmel, and the prophets of Baal four hundred and fifty, and the prophets of the groves four hundred, which eat at Jezebel's table. 20 So Ahab sent unto all the children of Israel, and gathered the prophets together unto mount Carmel. 21

And Elijah came unto all the people, and
said, How long halt ye between two
opinions? If the LORD be God, follow him:
but if Baal, then follow him. And the people
answered him not a word. 22 Then said
Elijah unto the people, I, even I only, remain
a prophet of the LORD; but Baal's prophets
are four hundred and fifty men. 23 Let them
therefore give us two bullocks; and let them
choose one bullock for themselves, and cut
it in pieces, and lay it on wood, and put no
fire under: and I will dress the other bullock,
and lay it on wood, and put no fire under: 24
And call ye on the name of your gods, and I
will call on the name of the LORD: and the
God that answereth by fire, let him be God.
And all the people answered and said, It is
well spoken. 25 And Elijah said unto the
prophets of Baal, Choose you one bullock
for yourselves, and dress it first; for ye are
many; and call on the name of your gods,
but put no fire under. 26 And they took the
bullock which was given them, and they
dressed it, and called on the name of Baal
from morning even until noon, saying, O
Baal, hear us. But there was no voice, nor
any that answered. And they leaped upon
the altar which was made. 27 And it came to
pass at noon, that Elijah mocked them, and
said, Cry aloud: for he is a god; either he is

talking, or he is pursuing, or he is in a journey, or peradventure he sleepeth, and must be awaked. 28 And they cried aloud, and cut themselves after their manner with knives and lancets, till the blood gushed out upon them. 29 And it came to pass, when midday was past, and they prophesied until the time of the offering of the evening sacrifice, that there was neither voice, nor any to answer, nor any that regarded. 30 And Elijah said unto all the people, Come near unto me. And all the people came near unto him. And he repaired the altar of the LORD that was broken down. 31 And Elijah took twelve stones, according to the number of the tribes of the sons of Jacob, unto whom the word of the LORD came, saying, Israel shall be thy name: 32 And with the stones he built an altar in the name of the LORD: and he made a trench about the altar, as great as would contain two measures of seed. 33 And he put the wood in order, and cut the bullock in pieces, and laid him on the wood, and said, Fill four barrels with water, and pour it on the burnt sacrifice, and on the wood. 34 And he said, Do it the second time. And they did it the second time. And he said, Do it the third time. And they did it the third time. 35 And the water ran round about the altar; and he filled the trench also with water. 36 And it came to pass at the time of the offering of the evening sacrifice, that Elijah the prophet came near, and said, LORD God of Abraham, Isaac, and of Israel, let it be known this day that thou art God in Israel, and that I am thy servant, and that I have done all these things at thy word. 37 Hear me, O LORD, hear me, that this people may know that thou art the LORD God, and that thou hast turned their heart back again. 38 Then the fire of the LORD fell, and consumed the burnt sacrifice, and the wood, and the stones, and the dust, and licked up the water that was in the trench. 39 And when all the people saw it, they fell on their faces: and they said, The LORD, he is the God; the LORD, he is the God. 40 And Elijah said unto them, Take the prophets of Baal; let not one of them escape. And they took them: and Elijah brought them down to the brook Kishon, and slew them there.

Baal never answered! Even though Elijah mocked the Prophets of Baal and made fun of their god they never attacked Elijah. When it was time for Elijah to call upon the true God of Heaven that God answered with fire! He sent enough fire to consume the sacrifice, the soaking wet wood, the stones, the dust, and the water that was in the trench surrounding the alter. Now that is some fire power!

God answered with fire from above, but not just a lightning bolt that started some dry wood on fire that casually burnt a sacrifice like hot dogs on a campfire. This was more like a massive blow torch igniting from Heaven and consuming everything combustible and non-combustible! It was like an incinerator but open and uncontained yet still focused on the object and purpose, to show the God of Heaven able, and the false god Baal unable! Elijah was confident that God was able!

Shadrach, Meshach, and Abednego believed God was able!

In another Bible story about fire, this one found in Daniel chapter three, the people were ordered to bow down and worship the King. Failure to worship King Nebuchadnezzar would bring the punishment of being thrown alive into the fiery furnace basically burning them to death. This story is about the three Hebrew captives who refused to worship the King!

Shadrach, Meshach, and Abednego, the three Hebrews, said to the King...

> Daniel 3:17 If it be so, our God whom we serve is able to deliver us from the burning

fiery furnace, and he will deliver us out of thine hand, O king.

Shadrach, Meshach, and Abednego were already given a second chance by the King to worship him, but they would not. The King was furious with their answer, ordered the furnace to be heated seven times hotter than normal, and ordered them to be thrown into the furnace! The fire was so hot that the men who were throwing the guys into the furnace were killed by the heat and flames!

God did not protect them from being thrown into the furnace. He did something even more amazing! God did something that no King could ever do; something no powerful government in the world today can do; something that only God is able to do! God kept the heat and the flames from Shadrach, Meshach, and Abednego! The fiery furnace had absolutely no effect on the three men or the fourth man either!

What about the fourth man in the furnace? Yes, the Bible says they threw three men into the furnace, but they looked and saw four, and the fourth was like the Son of God! Not only were the three men not affected by the exceedingly hot furnace, God was in there Himself to be with them! The only things that were affected by the fire were the ropes that bound them!

King Nebuchadnezzar called Shadrach, Meshach, and Abednego out of the fire when he realized that their God was really God! What the Bible says next is the finishing touch that only God could provide. This is unbelievable!

> Daniel 3:26-27 Then Nebuchadnezzar came near to the mouth of the burning fiery furnace, and spake, and said, Shadrach, Meshach, and Abednego, ye servants of the most high God, come forth, and come hither. Then Shadrach, Meshach, and Abednego, came forth of the midst of the fire. 27 And the princes, governors, and captains, and the king's counsellors, being gathered together, saw these men, <u>upon whose bodies the fire had no power, nor was an hair of their head singed, neither were their coats changed, nor the smell of fire had passed on them.</u>

Not a singed hair, not one! No burns on their clothes, none! Not even the smell of smoke was on them! That is really unbelievable, and I wouldn't believe it except that God was involved! I mean this is unreal! Every time I go to a campfire I try to sit upwind, but at the end of the night I still smell like smoke. Even if I just go to someone's house and they have a fire in a fireplace or in a wood burner in the basement I still smell like smoke! Just a little smoke from my wood burning kit when I was a kid made me smell like smoke. The Bible doesn't say, but my guess is that King Nebuchadnezzar probably smelled like smoke because he was near the furnace. Shadrach, Meshach, and Abednego did not even smell like smoke, and they were in the furnace! God really showed some ability there!

Jesus, God in the flesh, displayed ability! Jesus feeds 5000!

Most people know that Jesus feed 5000 people in a desert place but sometimes they don't know how He did it. The God of Creation now in human form was able to feed 5000 men plus women and children from just five loaves of bread and two fish. When we include their wives and children in the head count there could have been 15000 people there that day. Even at 5000 people present this is a huge miracle. These five loaves were not MEGA loaves and the fish were not humpback whales, this was a lunch that a boy was willing to share with Jesus and the people; regular fish and regular loaves.

Whenever we have unexpected guests for dinner we do the best we can to feed everybody with the food we thought we were going to eat. We open another can of green beans, maybe some canned fruit. We cut the meat into smaller portions, and if we have time we mash a couple of extra potatoes. Maybe we will even add some leftover food from the fridge to get by. Jesus had none of these options nor did He need them!

As the disciples distributed the food Jesus kept multiplying it until everybody ate and was satisfied. Some people try to figure out how you could divide fish and bread into such small portions instead of trying to figure out how Jesus stretched this little bit of food to feed so many people. The miracle was in the multiplication. When they collected the left overs they had much more than they started with AND everyone was full!

The ability to multiply the food source was miraculous. God's influence over material things shows His ability to not only make something out of nothing like He did at creation, but also His ability to make much out of little!

Peter was able walk on the water, because of Jesus!

Jesus sent His disciples in a boat to the other side of the sea while He stayed behind. The Disciples (including Peter) were trying to get across but the wind was contrary and the waves were against them. The guys were working hard and not getting to their destination. The stormy seas were just too much for them.

The Bible says Jesus came to them...walking on the water! I can say that I have walked on water too, but not like this! I have walked across frozen lakes dozens of times in my life. In fact I drove that wonderful big truck I had across a lake or two to fetch my broken snowmobile! I have never walked on top of "liquid" water like Jesus did. People can't normally walk on water we're not buoyant enough to stay on top. We drop into the water.

We would think if anybody could walk on the water it would have to be God. In this case it was Jesus. Logic then says that that He who does the impossible, Jesus, is God. Moses walked across the Red Sea but on the dry sea floor. Joshua walked across the Jordan River but on the dry river bed. Neither was on the water. Jesus walked across the Sea of Galilee ON the water!

We can probably agree that if God is God then He can walk anywhere He wants to walk, including on the water. Look now at what Jesus is able to do for Peter!

> Matthew 14:28-29 And Peter answered him and said, Lord, if it be thou, bid me come unto thee on the water. 29 And he said, Come. And when Peter was come down out

of the ship, he walked on the water, to go to Jesus.

Jesus has the ability to let Peter also walk on water! Peter is just another man. He has no special abilities! As they say, he puts his pants on one leg at a time just like we do. The ability was in Jesus! Jesus allowed Peter to defy the laws of nature and walk on the water through faith in Him. When Peter was distracted by the wind and the waves he began to sink, immediately again Peter trusted Jesus to save him! That is a very important point; Peter was able to do something that people cannot do because of the ability of Jesus! Peter trusted Jesus, and Jesus was and is able to deliver, able to save!

Why is Jesus able to save?

Just as God has the power to help Moses, Joshua, Elijah, and peter. He has the power and ability to intervene in our lives and help us! He is able! Jesus has the power over life and death because He is God, and He is able. The Bible says...

> John 10:17-18 Therefore doth my Father love me, because I lay down my life, that I might take it again. 18 No man taketh it from me, but I lay it down of myself. I have power to lay it down, and I have power to

<u>take it again.</u> This commandment have I received of my Father.

Jesus lived and died here on this earth. He was buried and rose again from the grave! He paid the penalty for all our sins; all the sins for all the people! When He died, He did so voluntarily of His own free will. Only He had the power to do that, He is able!

Chapter Five

"Need More Light"

I remember the first house I ever bought; it was a real 'fixer-upper'. There were a lot of positives with the property. There were nice shade trees, and it was on a lake in the country. The lake was good for speed boats and skiing, snorkeling, and fishing. It was just big enough but not too big, just busy enough but not too busy. The property was small but beautiful.

The house itself needed help, but I bought it anyway. I was a bit of a handyman and the important things with the house were good. The foundation was still solid, the walls stood straight and true, and the roofline was straight as an arrow. There was no sway in that roof even though it was due for new shingles. Inside was decorated in UGLY. All the trim wood that was still there was painted flat black, and the baseboards were all brown. There was dark brown paneling in all the rooms except the ones that had dark green paneling (no lie). The kitchen was the only room that was decent. The cupboards were fairly nice but dark oak, and the walls were drywall with yellow paint on them.

The floors were mostly carpeted. The carpet was very dark brown cut pile, and some of it was carpet squares. One room had dark orange shag carpet which was the first thing to go! The kitchen had a nice piece of linoleum that kind of matched the yellow walls. It was installed crooked so the pattern was out of line with the cupboards, but not too far off.

There was a light fixture in the kitchen and in the bathroom and that was it. Every other room had a light bulb hanging from a wire dangling somewhere near the center of the room. This produced a shadowy light that was bright in a few areas and the rest was dim and dingy.

As a single guy I had no problem moving in there as it was, but it was no place for a wife and family. It took everything I had to get the down payment and the first few months mortgage paid. It was dim and dark but it was mine and I was going to fix it up.

Without much cash to start with I started to make and prioritize my plans for the house makeover that I knew would take me several years. I cleaned and evaluated everything. What I thought was good I would keep, and what I thought was really not so good I would remodel.

As I began to get on top of things I thought that a little paint would go a long way in brightening things up! I began covering the flat black paint with semi-gloss white and the brown baseboards would become a lighter tan. I was excited enough that the fact that it took three coats of the light colors to cover the dark colors didn't even bother me. I was surprised how much difference that light trim made!

An unanticipated consequence of the new paint was the lighter trim quickly showed how dingy and dark that old paneling was. As time went on I eventually got the money together to buy paint for the paneling. I knew other young homeowners who faced a similar problem. Paint did the trick for them, why not try it! Before I was going to paint all the walls I wanted better light so I replaced all the 40 watt bulbs with 100's! Whew! I loved the light but that extra light showed me something. Three walls of the living room were real wood paneling but the fourth wall was that cheap chip board kind with the plastic 'look like' wood cover on it. The extra light revealed something I never noticed, plastic un-paintable paneling.

Then I noticed the carpet. What I thought was going to be acceptable really was not. There were bare spots and burn marks, and over by the sliding glass door the carpet had faded into a completely different color! Every time I upgraded in one area it just shed light on a new problem, and that's the way it went for years until I finally got everything up to standard.

When I began to lighten things up inside my 'fixer-upper' I found out it was worse than I thought. Knowledge is like that light that I applied to my old living room. When you don't know much about the situation that you are in, your circumstances may not seem so bad. The more light you shed on the subject the more you see the dirt, the cracks, the burn marks and the old faded carpet. You begin to realize what is good and bad; what you can keep, and what you need to replace.

In life, what you know directly impacts the way you respond to situations and questions. You might make a good decision or you might make a bad decision. It all depends how much light you have on it. Perspective is vital. You cannot have the proper perspective without knowledge of the subject. You cannot have knowledge of a subject without encountering it in some way. You cannot make an informed decision while you are uninformed, but when you are informed the decision is much easier and maybe even obvious!

Here are the stories of three real life people who encountered a situation, gathered sufficient information, then made an informed decision; a decision that became obvious to them.

The Woman at the Well

Let's look to John 4 and the story of the Woman at the Well. The scene of the story is in Samaria at a water well that Jacob gave to Joseph's family long before. Judea was in the southern part of Israel and Galilee was in the northern area. Samaria was located directly in between the two. The Orthodox Jews didn't like the Samaritans at all and wanted to avoid them as much as possible. Samaritans were not purely Jewish, but they were of mixed heritage; Jews and Gentiles together.

Jesus, coming from Judea heading toward Galilee had a choice of three basic routes. Many people of that day would go east to the Jordan River and cross before turning north to go to Galilee, thereby avoiding Samaria completely. Another option was to go along the Mediterranean Sea Coast also avoiding Samaria. Of course the third option was to travel directly through Samaria. It was a more direct route, shorter and quicker! Jesus didn't care too much what the Scribes and Pharisees thought and decided to cut right through Samaria.

Along the way, Jesus meets a Samaritan woman at a well, a worldly woman we will find out. Jesus strikes up a conversation with her...

> John 4:5-7 Then cometh He to a city of Samaria, which is called Sychar, near to the

parcel of ground that Jacob gave to his son Joseph. 6 Now Jacob's well was there. Jesus therefore, being wearied with his journey, sat thus on the well: and it was about the sixth hour. 7 There cometh a woman of Samaria to draw water: Jesus saith unto her, Give me to drink.

Evidently she is not shy and she enters a conversation with Him.

John 4:9 Then saith the woman of Samaria unto him, How is it that thou, being a Jew, askest drink of me, which am a woman of Samaria? for the Jews have no dealings with the Samaritans.

Within the culture there Jesus had two reasons why he shouldn't talk to this woman. First, He was a man, and second, He was a Jew. The Samaritan woman was interested. She must have thought; "Why are you talking to me? You want me to get you a drink? Don't you know that you're not supposed to want to be anywhere near me?" The Samaritan Woman immediately took from the conversation that Jesus was not just another Jew. Jesus was socially indifferent.

The conversation continues...

John 4:10-12 Jesus answered and said unto her, If thou knewest the gift of God, and who it is that saith to thee, Give me to drink; thou wouldest have asked of Him, and He would have given thee living water. 11 The woman saith unto Him, Sir, thou hast nothing to draw with, and the well is deep: from whence then hast thou that living water? 12 Art thou greater than our father Jacob, which gave us the well, and drank thereof himself, and his children, and his cattle?

Jesus tells her that if she knew who He was, and what He could give her she would ask for it. If she had enough light on the subject she would know what to choose! Jesus metaphorically refers to "gift of God" as "living water," and it is something only God can give. Romans 6:23 says at the end of the verse, "the gift of God is eternal life through Jesus Christ our Lord". Jesus is telling her that He is the Lord who can give this gift!

The Samaritan Woman misses the metaphor and wonders where Jesus gets this "living water". He has nothing to dip from the well with. She doesn't get it yet, but she is still seeking an answer. She reflects on the origin of the water well. Jacob gave this well, and Jacob has been supplying water to these people for nearly two thousand years, are you greater than he? Can you top that Jesus?

> John 4:13-15 Jesus answered and said unto her, Whosoever drinketh of this water shall thirst again: 14 But whosoever drinketh of the water that I shall give him shall never thirst; but the water that I shall give him shall be in him a well of water springing up into everlasting life. 15 The woman saith unto him, Sir, give me this water, that I thirst not, neither come hither to draw.

Jesus is explaining the word picture He is drawing here. This physical water will help you temporarily, but the spiritual water, the Living Water, is eternal life! Eternal life is what you need, but the Woman has not quite solved the riddle and is almost ignorantly challenging Jesus "give me this water". She was coming to understand but not completely. If Jesus can give better water than Jacob she wants it, whatever it means. She begins to believe that Jesus has something to give that no one else has.

Jesus shifts gears in the coming verses...

> John 4:16-19 Jesus saith unto her, Go, call thy husband, and come hither. 17 The woman answered and said, I have no husband. Jesus said unto her, Thou hast well said, I have no husband: 18 For thou hast had five husbands; and he whom thou now hast is not thy husband: in that saidst thou

truly. 19 The woman saith unto him, Sir, I perceive that thou art a prophet.

Jesus tells her of her sordid past. She has had five husbands and the one she now has is not her husband. She says, "Sir, I perceive that thou art a prophet." Now she realizes some more about Jesus. He has extraordinary abilities.

She has come down a pathway of belief finding that Jesus was not just another Jew, that He might have something to give that no one else can give, and that He possessed incredible ability. She thought that He was at the very least, a prophet. We find that she believes in the coming Messiah as most of the Samaritans did, although she does not yet realize that she is talking to Him.

> John 4:25 The woman saith unto him, I know that Messias cometh, which is called Christ: when he is come, he will tell us all things.

She has been getting closer and closer to the truth, now she seems ready to hear it straight out.

> John 4:26 Jesus saith unto her, I that speak unto thee am He.

The Woman had been building up knowledge that would enable her to accept the obvious. That Jesus is the Messiah, the One she believed would come.

She had encountered someone who, in her mind, went from a total stranger to Messiah! When she realized WHO Jesus was she immediately went to tell everybody she could find, she became a witness!

> John 4:39-42 And many of the Samaritans of that city believed on him for the saying of the woman, which testified, He told me all that ever I did. 40 So when the Samaritans were come unto him, they besought him that he would tarry with them: and he abode there two days. 41 And many more believed because of his own word; 42 And said unto the woman, Now we believe, not because of thy saying: for we have heard him ourselves, and know that this is indeed the Christ, the Savior of the world.

The light of the Savior shone greater and greater onto the Woman at the well, and her understanding grew as she learned. She became a witness the people of Samaria! They came to see what she was talking about. They learned for themselves with an open mind, and they understood Jesus as Savior!

What about the Centurion at the Crucifixion of Jesus?

Crucifixion is an ugly thing, brutal and without compassion. One of the most torturous avenues of death anyone could ever encounter. The men who carried out these gruesome executions had to be hard, unemotional, and personally detached from their work. I would think that carrying out crucifixion after crucifixion, week after week, for time unending would drive any caring and compassionate man insane. Only the callous uncaring heart could crucify another. Possibly after a certain number of crucifixions, for those Roman Soldiers, it would be just like another day at the office. These men had to be the hardest of the hard!

I am also sure they had seen it all when it comes to those they were executing. Some would die at the beatings before they ever get to the cross. Some would beg for their lives. Others would try to fight free. Maybe some would hurl insults back at the soldiers or at those who mocked them. Some would die quickly while others would linger, clinging to life. They would break the legs of some to get them to die quicker while inflicting the most possible pain in the meantime. The cold heartless Roman Soldiers carrying out these executions had been there and done that. Nothing would faze them. They were killing machines carrying out orders, processing criminals as cruelly and inhumanely as possible.

Roman soldiers believed in rank and file authority. They would follow orders no matter how cruel and heartless they might be. They believed in, discipline, battle formations, armor, and weapons. They kept tactical advantage in all situations, and if they ever had a doubt they never showed it.

Jesus' crucifixion would have not been anything special to them. The guilty criminals were turned over to them for execution, and the soldiers were just following orders. To them, Jesus was just another criminal about to get His justice. There had been others who "said" they were the Messiah as Jesus did[1], Jesus' claim to be the Son of God wasn't even unique to these men[2].

The Centurion in charge of this group of men would have been time tested and battle hardened. He would have worked his way up the chain of command to the point where he commanded his own group of soldiers. He was taking orders from the high command yet giving orders to his men. Possibly this Centurion would have carried out these crucifixion activities in his younger years. He would have had experience in these matters from years of service. Practically nothing would faze him. Supernaturally, something was about to frighten

95

this mighty warrior and cause him to make an unlikely acknowledgement.

Jesus' composure throughout the crucifixion process was uncharacteristic of the men who were usually killed there. Jesus never fought back; not physically, not verbally, not at all. Even though it would have been hopeless for one normal man to physically challenge a Roman Centurion and his guard I'm sure normal men did. They must have tried to run or get away somehow. Jesus didn't resist, didn't hurl insults, didn't curse, and never even swore.

In fact, the things Jesus did say were not mean spirited at all. He said, "Father, forgive them; for they know not what they do[3]", and words of forgiveness to the repentant criminal on the cross next to him, "Verily I say unto thee, Today shalt thou be with me in paradise[4]".

What Jesus did not say from the cross would have spoken just as loudly to the Roman Centurion. The people who were there (the soldiers, the townspeople, and even one of the criminals hanging on a cross next to Jesus) were all sneering at Jesus.

> Luke 23:35-39 And the people stood beholding. And the rulers also with them derided him, saying, He saved others; let

him save himself, if he be Christ, the chosen of God. 36 And the soldiers also mocked him, coming to him, and offering him vinegar, 37 And saying, If thou be the king of the Jews, save thyself. 38 And a superscription also was written over him in letters of Greek, and Latin, and Hebrew, THIS IS THE KING OF THE JEWS. 39 And one of the malefactors which were hanged railed on him, saying, If thou be Christ, save thyself and us.

They were insulting, mocking, and verbally abusing Jesus yet He didn't return insult for insult, nor did He in any way abuse any of them.

No doubt the Roman Centurion realizes that there is a difference between this person and all the others that he has put to death. If he didn't know at this point that it was a supernatural Jesus that was able to keep His composure through this ordeal, he was about to find out. I want to focus on three of the things that the Centurion would have understood as abnormal.

First, there was darkness from the sixth hour until the ninth hour. In our terms that would be from noon to 3pm, when the sun in normally the highest in the sky. As Jesus hung on the cross the sun was obscured and there was darkness for three hours. I don't know how God did it. Certainly these ancient people would have known about solar eclipses, and they also would realize that eclipses don't last for three hours. The point is that it happened supernaturally. I can't explain it nor do I have to. It happened.

Secondly, there was a great earthquake just as Jesus was giving up his Spirit. Earthquakes happen all around the earth and can happen at any time of day or night. This quake happened right on cue. Three hours of darkness and an earth quake simultaneous with Christ's death was no coincidence and the Roman Centurion knew it.

The veil in the temple was torn from top to bottom. This is a very spiritually significant event. This huge and very thick fabric curtain could not be torn by any human hands, it was far too strong. The veil kept a barrier between sinful men and Holy God. At that moment Jesus had fulfilled the punishment for the sins of mankind and the veil was no longer needed. I am mentioning it because of its significance, but I cannot argue that the Centurion knew of or understood what the tearing of the veil meant, so this is not my third point.

The third thing the Roman Centurion did notice was how Jesus transitioned from physical life to physical death. Luke 23:46 says,

> Luke 23:46 And when Jesus had cried with a loud voice, he said, Father, into thy hands I commend my spirit: and having said thus, he gave up the ghost.

Jesus was actually and noticeably in control of when He would die. Read Jesus' words in the gospel of John.

> John 10:17-18 Therefore doth my Father love me, because I lay down my life, that I might take it again. 18 No man taketh it from me, but I lay it down of myself. I have power to lay it down, and I have power to take it again. This commandment have I received of my Father.

Jesus had the power to lay down His life and power to take it back up, and he displayed this power in full view of that Roman Centurion!

From the Centurion's point of view, he came to work that day to carry out some executions. This was something he had done many times before. He encountered a prisoner who was noticeably different; never trying to escape, never yelling abusive language toward anybody, and consistently displaying nothing but forgiveness. He encountered circumstances beyond reason; the darkness in the afternoon, the earthquake, and the way Jesus was even in control of the exact time of His death.

What was the Centurion's response to these events he was witnessing? How did the facts of the case of Jesus change the Centurion's thinking? Scripture tells us. We can find a complete answer from just three passages.

> Matthew 27:54 Now when the centurion, and they that were with him, watching Jesus, saw the earthquake, and those things that were done, they feared greatly, saying, Truly this was the Son of God.

> Mark 15:39 And when the centurion, which stood over against him, saw that he so cried out, and gave up the ghost, he said, Truly this man was the Son of God.

> Luke 23:47-48 Now when the centurion saw what was done, he glorified God, saying, Certainly this was a righteous man. 48 And all the people that came together to that sight, beholding the things which were done, smote their breasts, and returned.

From these passages you can truly see the effect of Jesus on the Centurion AND those who were watching. They could not deny what their eyes had seen! The Matthew passage says they "feared greatly". This is the tried and true killing machine that was in charge of men of war, and he "feared greatly". This man who was not afraid of anything was led to exclaim something that could have gotten him executed, "Truly this was the Son of God!" At this point he was more afraid of what God might do than what the Roman Command would do.

As the Roman Centurion gathered evidence about Jesus, it was like more and more light being shown on Jesus. As the Centurion saw more and more, he was better able to more clearly evaluate for himself who Jesus was.

I cannot say from these passages whether the Roman Centurion came all the way into a trusting relationship with the Savior that day. If he didn't trust Jesus for Salvation he should have. Legend has it that he did go on to be a proclaimer of the Gospel of Jesus Christ, but it is only legend. I cannot document it. It would make good sense though. When anyone comes to terms with who Jesus is they must decide to follow Him or not. That is obvious.

The Rich Man (and Lazarus)

By the time some people get enough light on the subject of Jesus to make the obvious choice it is too late. Only after the chance at salvation has passed by do they finally understand. I think this is where the majority of people will find themselves, but there is no reason that you have to be one of them. The Rich Man in this story wouldn't want you to realize what the obvious choice is too late, like he did.

The story is found in Luke 16. Jesus is the story teller. It is the story of Lazarus and the Rich Man. Read through it with a focus on the Rich Man, his attitudes, practices, and his goals.

> Luke 16:19-31 There was a certain rich man, which was clothed in purple and fine linen, and fared sumptuously every day: 20 And there was a certain beggar named Lazarus, which was laid at his gate, full of sores, 21 And desiring to be fed with the crumbs which fell from the rich man's table: moreover the dogs came and licked his sores. 22 And it came to pass, that the beggar died, and was carried by the angels into Abraham's bosom: the rich man also died, and was buried; 23 And in hell he lift up his eyes, being in torments, and seeth Abraham afar off, and Lazarus in his bosom. 24 And he cried and said, Father Abraham, have mercy on me, and send Lazarus, that he may dip the tip of his finger in water, and cool my tongue; for I am tormented in this flame. 25 But Abraham said, Son, remember that thou in thy lifetime receivedst thy good

things, and likewise Lazarus evil things: but now he is comforted, and thou art tormented. 26 And beside all this, between us and you there is a great gulf fixed: so that they which would pass from hence to you cannot; neither can they pass to us, that would come from thence. 27 Then he said, I pray thee therefore, father, that thou wouldest send him to my father's house: 28 For I have five brethren; that he may testify unto them, lest they also come into this place of torment. 29 Abraham saith unto him, They have Moses and the prophets; let them hear them. 30 And he said, Nay, father Abraham: but if one went unto them from the dead, they will repent. 31 And he said unto him, If they hear not Moses and the prophets, neither will they be persuaded, though one rose from the dead.

The Rich Man had a problem and he didn't even realize it, he trusted his eternal soul to a "religious system" that could not save him instead of a living God who could! He seemed to think that he was rich enough, important enough, and therefore good enough to go to Heaven when he would die. He wore the good clothes and ate the finest meals; surely God would want him in Heaven because he "was" the upper class!

Obviously the poor, sick, beggar named Lazarus had put his trust and faith purely in God, we find him in Paradise or Heaven with Abraham. Abraham is the Patriarch of Israel, he was known as a friend[4] of God because of his faith in God.

> Galatians 3:7-9 Know ye therefore that <u>they which are of faith</u>, the same are the children of <u>Abraham</u>. 8 And the scripture, <u>foreseeing that God would justify the heathen through faith</u>, preached before the gospel unto <u>Abraham</u>, saying, In thee shall all nations be blessed. 9 So then <u>they which be of faith are blessed with faithful Abraham.</u>   *Underline mine*

Jesus is saying here that Lazarus is being blessed with faithful Abraham. They are together in Paradise. Therefore the Rich Man had to have put his personal faith in God to save him. By implication Jesus is saying that the rich man was not rich enough, not important enough, and not trusting in the right thing so he is in Hades, or Hell, paying for his own sins.

From his position in Hell the Rich Man looks up and sees the one who he would ignore by his gate, Lazarus. He asks if that filthy beggar could come comfort him in his flames by touching his tongue with a drop of water. I would say the Rich Man's perspective on what is important, and what is not, has changed. His fine purple clothes, clothes of importance and wealth, were not so important to him anymore. All his money could not help him nor his influential friends. Suddenly one man he routinely ignored as unimportant became his great hope.

There was no hope there however. Abraham explained how things work after this earthly life. Those who have put their faith and trust in God while on earth are sorted out from all those who did not, and there is no mixing, no trading, no passports, and no ticket booths to buy your ride out of there. When you die in your earthly life your status is forever set and it has nothing to do with economics, politics, or stature. It is simply based on where your faith and trust lies.

The Rich Man quickly realizes that it is too late for him. His fate is sealed. "I pray thee therefore, father, that thou wouldest send him to my father's house: For I have five brethren; that he may testify unto them, lest they also come into this place of torment" was the Rich Man's urgent cry! He clearly does not want those he loves to follow the same path as he did. Just between you and me, I wouldn't want my worst enemy to go to Hell let alone a friend or family member. I agree with the Rich Man on this point! Maybe you agree with him too!

Abraham explains "They have Moses and the prophets; let them hear them". In other words the Rich Man's family has the complete revealed Word of God for that time. They should follow His Word and trust Him. We have discovered the reliability of God's Word while were still in our earthly life, the Rich Man found it after he died. The choice to follow the Word of God became Obvious to him, but too late.

The Rich Man cries out again, "but if one went unto them from the dead, they will repent". It is now obvious to him that he made the wrong choices in life and desperately wants his loved ones to avoid eternity in Hell. As Abraham says at the end of the passage; "If they will not respond to God's Word, they won't respond to one who rose from the dead." The Obvious choice to have faith and trust in God has passed the Rich Man by.

You might be thinking to yourself, "If somebody came up from the dead and told me that God, Heaven, and Hell were really real I would defiantly believe them and worship God in faith." Well, somebody did come from the dead to give you the truth about Heaven and Hell. His name is Jesus. After He died He rose on the third day and was subsequently seen by literally hundreds of people. At that time the revealed Word of God was still being written and the Holy Spirit has testified through human writers in the New Testament Scriptures. The choice now is more obvious than ever. Jesus is the Christ, and we need to trust and have faith in Him alone to save us from our sinful ways, before we end up with the Rich Man.

[1] Matthew 26:64, Mark 14:62, Luke 22:70

[2] Flavius Josephus, *Antiquities* Book 18 Chapter 1

[3] Luke 23:34

[4] James 2:23

Chapter Six

It's Obvious Who "I AM"

What did Jesus say and how did He back it up?

There are some people that we all know, but we've never met. Let me be more specific. We know about them. We know what they did or what they said even though we might not know them personally. Even if somehow we've never heard of these people we know someone who knows about them. Sooner or later we will hear of them!

I'll mention a couple so I can show you what I mean. Let's start with an easy one, Michael Jackson. With the exception of a very few people who will read this book, we have never personally met Michael Jackson, and still we all know him. We have heard of his work, we have seen the excitement of his devoted followers. We believe he existed; although he is gone now. Odds are that you know Michael Jackson.

You might be thinking, "I don't get it." Obviously we know Michael Jackson, and we have recordings of his voice, movies, and videos bearing his image. We even have news footage showing Michael in real life situations. There are plenty of us alive today who physically saw the "King of Pop" at a concert or on the street as he exited his vehicle. There are thousands and thousands of people all around the world, speaking in dozens of languages, who would gladly share their story of encounter with Michael Jackson even if it was just a brief passing in the airport.

What about someone you've never seen before? You've never passed by them in the airport much less see them arrive in a limousine. Think about Michelangelo or William Shakespeare. We might have seen an artist's sketch of them but never a photograph. We don't have a recording of their voices so we can't say we've heard them speak. History tells us where and when they lived, but they are gone now. Both of these men left a body of work to the world that caused us to know them hundreds of years after they lived. Today there are thousands of people who would testify how the work of these men gave them great joy or inspired them in some way. No one would ever try to say that they didn't exist. It is obvious that they did!

All three of these men did their work out in the open, at the time they lived it was known what they did, they were known by their doings. Their popularity seemed to grow after they died, all three are worth more today than when they were alive. There is evidence showing their existence and overwhelmingly today we believe they were here. It's obvious!

The most famous person ever is not Michael Jackson (although he is famous worldwide). Neither is it Michelangelo who painted and sculpted his way to great notoriety. And while Shakespeare's plays are now movies, he is not on top of this list. The most famous person of this or any era is none other than Jesus Christ. In fact, Jesus stands alone as the central, most historically prominent person that ever lived. The name of Jesus is known worldwide today. There might be some people somewhere who have never heard the name of Jesus, but before it is all said and done everyone who ever lived will know about Jesus.

> Philippians 2:9-11 Wherefore God also hath highly exalted him, and given him a name which is above every name: 10 That at the name of Jesus every knee should bow, of things in heaven, and things in earth, and things under the earth; 11 And that every tongue should confess that Jesus Christ is Lord, to the glory of God the Father.

Whether accepted or rejected, Jesus Christ is known for what He said and for what He did. Jesus was, and still is today, very open and upfront about why He is relevant to our lives. In this book we have already established that the Bible really is God's Word, and that we can rely on what it says. We can look at what Jesus said and believe it is true. We can look at what others in the Bible have said and believe that their words are true as well because of the inspiration of the Holy Spirit. Therefore, we can draw a conclusion from the truth we read and make an obvious choice.

To understand what Jesus said about who He is I want to introduce you to a little ancient Greek phrase that Jesus used over and over again, εγω ειμι, or as we would write it with English characters, ego eimi, which means "I, I am". The Greek word εγω or ego, is a personal pronoun that is translated "I". The word ει   I or eimi is a verb meaning "I am". You can say "I am" by simply saying "ειμι" but the Lord Jesus combined it with the word εγώ several times to emphasize what He is saying, "I and only I am"

In the speech of the first century it would have been clear to the listeners that Jesus was saying that He was God. For the Jewish citizens and ruling leaders the expression that Jesus used would have triggered a memory of what they had all known from their history.

Moses asked God at the event of the burning bush in Exodus 3 about His name, here is what God said

> Exodus 3:13-14 And Moses said unto God, Behold, when I come unto the children of Israel, and shall say unto them, The God of your fathers hath sent me unto you; and they shall say to me, What is his name? what shall I say unto them? 14 And God said unto Moses, I AM THAT I AM: and he said, Thus shalt thou say unto the children of Israel, I AM hath sent me unto you.

What is rendered here as "I am that I am" is from the same phrase, εγω ειμι, as is written in the Greek translation of the Old Testament. I don't want to get completely lost in a discussion of translations. I would rather make a point with which almost all Bible Scholars agree. When Jesus said "I, I AM" the Jewish population of first century Israel understood that He was calling Himself God by drawing on the name that God Himself gave of Himself to their beloved Moses at the burning bush.

Jesus is emphasizing that He is God. He does some things that are recorded in Scripture to make it obvious to us that He is God! In John chapter 6 Jesus does an incredible miracle. While out in the middle of nowhere Jesus feeds the 5000 men from five loaves and two small fish. These five loaves were not MEGA Loaves and the fish were not humpback whales. This was a lunch that a boy carried and was willing to share with Jesus and the people; regular fish and regular loaves.

Now keep in mind that this number represents 5000 men who were following Jesus. It is extremely likely that a great number of these men had wives and children, so we can conservatively guess that there were between 10,000 and 15,000 people represented at this meal! Even if we want to downsize it and say that it was just the men there are still 5000 of them!

I have been in a crowd of 5000 people before. A crowd that size takes up some space and eats a lot. In our home town of Kalamazoo there is a minor league hockey arena that seats 5,113 people. I have been there when it has been sold out. The concessions to feed that many people are massive. I've never counted them, but there must be fifteen or twenty food outlets around the concourse plus the restaurant underneath. Let me tell you something else, when they stock the concessions before a game they do it by the truck load, not by the picnic basket. That many people in one place eat a lot of food!

Jesus fed the 5000 with five loaves and two small fish; an extraordinary miracle. In fact Jesus did something that the hockey stadium could never do. He had his disciples pick up the scraps and there was a lot more there than they even started out with! Because Jesus is God He has no problem with miracles. The God who created everything can easily create a meal for that 5000 or more people!

The next day Jesus gave them a word picture taking the message of the miracle of the feeding and making a spiritual application for them to learn. The group followed Jesus to Capernaum and began a discussion with Jesus. To really make it brief, Jesus tells them that they followed him NOT because of the miracle but because HE fed them. They were enjoying the benefits of being around Jesus without believing Jesus is God.

The people sort of begin to negotiate with Jesus in a way. They said things like, "What sign do you show us Jesus?" "We need to see something of what are we believing in, if we see it then we can believe it!" "What is your sign today?" They conveniently avoid the miracle feeding just the day before, then they reflect on their heritage... Moses fed our fathers (read ancestors) manna, bread from Heaven. They all knew that Israel ate Manna for free, every day, for years and years and years.

The group of followers here are trying to incite Jesus to "one up" Moses. I can just hear them, "Hey Jesus, Moses fed us every day for forty years. You just fed us once so what are you going to do about that?" They want Jesus to prove Himself to be better than Moses, to do more than Moses. They want to eat for free. It is interesting how we as people try to manipulate God.

Jesus doesn't take the bait but responds with the truth He has been waiting to share. "I, and only I am the Bread of Life" he says in verse 35 of John 6. Jesus chooses to use the phrase "εγω ειμι", (ego eimi). This is the very phrase in Greek that is attributed to God only. When Moses asked who God was God said "I AM". "I AM" was the name by which the Jehovah God of Israel identified himself to Moses. Jesus' group of followers name dropped Moses trying to get some more free food. Jesus name dropped that He is God. By this He was showing them that He, and only He is the God of their beloved Moses. Jesus goes on to say in verses 47-48

> John 6:47-48 Verily, verily, I say unto you, He that believeth on Me hath everlasting life. I am that bread of life.

Again, Jesus says "ego eimi". "I and only I am the bread that gives life!" Jesus did the miracle and they wanted more because of their selfishness or laziness. Then He told them I am the God that gives life. Jesus Intentionally used the phrase signifying that He is God. It wasn't a mistake. Jesus was telling them and us that He is God!

The book of John records many of these statements that we have come to know as "I AM Statements of Christ". Each time Jesus says this He is pointing out the obvious to the audience; I Am God! Each time He says, "I AM", Jesus points out a truth about Himself. He says something that He wants to make obvious.

> John 6:35 And Jesus said unto them, I am the bread of life: he that cometh to me shall never hunger;
>
> John 6:48 I am that bread of life.
>
> John 6:51 I am the living bread which came down from heaven: if any man eat of this bread, he shall live for ever: (my underlines)

Bread or food sustains life in the realm of the earthlings. Just like food keeps our physical bodies going and growing, in the spiritual realm Jesus is the only thing that can feed our soul causing it to grow and thrive. He is the giver and sustainer of life.

> John 8:12 Then spake Jesus again unto them, saying, I am the light of the world: he that followeth me shall not walk in darkness, but shall have the light of life. (my underline)

Light shows us the way to go. The light of God's Word shows us how to walk in His ways and not be in the darkness of our sins. Psalm 119:105 says, "Thy word is a lamp unto my feet, and a light unto my path." The light shows us where the path is, and John 1 says that the Word of God is Jesus. He shows us the good way to go. That good way is to believe Him and accept Him for who He is and for what he has done.

> John 8:24 I said therefore unto you, that ye shall die in your sins: for if ye believe not that I am he, ye shall die in your sins. (my underline)

Simply put Jesus is saying, "I AM God, you both believe and trust in Me (Jesus) or you don't, if you don't you will die in your sins. This is really how simple it is."

> John 8:58 Jesus said unto them, Verily, verily, I say unto you, Before Abraham was, I am. (my underline)

Jesus says before Abraham was, (past tense), I AM! Even though Jesus lived on earth roughly 2000 years after Abraham, Jesus IS before Abraham WAS, because Jesus is God, and He has always existed Let's look back to John 1. Here Scripture says that Jesus is the Word and that the Word was already there with God, as God, when God created everything from nothing.

John the Apostle says,

> John 1:3 All things were made by him; and without him was not any thing made that was made.

It is no coincidence that John chapter one also refers to Jesus as "the life and light of men". In the same way that He is the Bread of Life and the Light of the World. God's Word is such an amazing piece of literature that it has to have been written by the inspiration of the Holy Spirit. No man under his own power could have ever written this.

Moving on…

> John 10:7-9 Then said Jesus unto them again, Verily, verily, I say unto you, I am the door of the sheep. 8 All that ever came before me are thieves and robbers: but the sheep did not hear them. 9 I am the door: by me if any man enter in, he shall be saved, and shall go in and out, and find pasture. (my underlines)

Jesus is God and "the Door". Doors protect us don't they? We close our doors to keep robbers out and to keep the bad weather that will harm us out.

Doors protect us. Jesus is our protection once we believe and trust in Him. He is our keeper. Jesus saves us and keeps us from the one who wants to devour us. He is someone else that everyone knows about; he is Satan or the Devil. The Bible says about him,

> 1 Peter 5:8 Be sober, be vigilant; because your adversary the devil, as a roaring lion, walketh about, seeking whom he may devour.

We have to be serious about this because the Devil wants to bring us down and ruin us. Jesus is the Door that protects us.

> John 10:11 I am the good shepherd: the good shepherd giveth his life for the sheep.
>
> John 10:14 I am the good shepherd, and know my sheep, and am known of mine. (my underlines)

Jesus has sacrificed Himself for us! He says, "I AM God and I give my life for my sheep". If we believe and trust in Him the Bible calls us His Sheep. He has given His life for us. If that is not exciting enough, in John 10:14 Jesus says, "I AM God and I know my sheep, and they know me!" WOW! The God of the Universe, the God that created everything that we see and everything that we cannot see, knows us!

And we can know Him! We know Him by knowing His Word. We see in the Bible knowing that His Word is Jesus Himself.

> John 11:25 Jesus said unto her, I am the resurrection, and the life: he that believeth in me, though he were dead, yet shall he live: (my underline)

At the grave of his friend Lazarus Jesus said, "I AM God the Resurrection and the Life". Jesus was raising Lazarus from the grave after Lazarus had been dead for four days. In just a few weeks Jesus would rise from the grave Himself on the third day after his own death by crucifixion. Again, Jesus stresses belief in Him as the means of Salvation.

> John 14:6 Jesus saith unto him, I am the way, the truth, and the life: no man cometh unto the Father, but by me. (my underline)

In John 14 Jesus is talking with His disciples and He says again, "I AM God! I AM the one and only way, I AM the one and only truth, I AM the one and only life. Nobody comes to the Father (or nobody will come into Heaven) except through me, Jesus--who is God."

> John 15:1 I am the true vine, and my Father is the husbandman.

> John 15:5 I am the vine, ye are the branches: He that abideth in me, and I in him, the same bringeth forth much fruit: for without me ye can do nothing. (my underline)

In John 15, Jesus is still talking with His disciples, and we hear Him saying, "I AM God and I am the vine. We believers are the branches. Branches cannot live very long if they are cut off of the vine because the vine sustains the life of the branch. So, apart from the vine we die. Grafted into the vine that will sustain us we will bear much fruit! It is obvious which is better, don't you think?

There is another thing about vines and branches that give us a good picture of how we should be responding to Jesus today. When the branch is grafted into the vine it takes nourishment from the vine. Over time the branch grows together with the vine and the two become inseparable. You can't take them apart because they have become part of each other.

In the book of Acts Jesus indicates who he is to Paul, who was then called Saul.

> Acts 9:5 And he said, Who art thou, Lord? And the Lord said I am Jesus whom thou persecutest: it is hard for

thee to kick against the pricks. (my underline)

Finally, Jesus confronts Saul of Tarsus who was trained in the ways of the Jewish Religion. He was a Pharisee. Saul sees a flash of light and hears a voice saying, "I AM God, I AM Jesus, the one you are persecuting. It is hard for you to go against me!" It wasn't a question. It was a statement. Saul could not succeed against Jesus because Jesus is God. Saul (along with any other reasonably well trained Jew of the day) would have immediately known the phrase "ego eimi" and known that the person saying it was equating themselves with God. Now Saul was hearing that phrase, not from another man standing in front of him, but he was hearing it from Heaven directly from the lips of God, Jesus, Himself.

Jesus was not shy about who He was then, and He is not shy about who He is today. He has told us exactly who He is in His revealed Word, and he has shown us what He has done for us. Through many proofs and evidences that we have already outlined in this book we have established that God's Word, the Bible, is reliable and that Jesus was not just a good man or even a great one, but that He is God.

We are now at the point that we realize that Jesus, God in the flesh, is not hiding from us. He is not playing a game. He is not saying that He might be

God if you will believe. He is God whether you believe it or not. He has told us exactly who He is! He is simply waiting for us to respond to Him.

Chapter Seven

Why is Jesus the Only Savior?

I can write this whole chapter in one sentence.

Jesus is able to save because of who He is, and because of what He has done.

Now I'm going to ask a really strange question that you might have to think about for a couple minutes. Do you know <u>what</u> the <u>who</u> of Jesus is? "Really?" you ask. I told you that you might have to think about it, so do that now. I'll wait for you.

Are you ready to press on? Good, me too! What I mean is, the "what" that Jesus "is" determines His eligibility to save us. That still sounds crazy doesn't it?

Jesus said he was God (as we outlined in the previous chapter), and He died for us saying that He was God. He stood there in a human body telling fiercely religious people, who knew of His earthly family, that He was God. People could see Him, and hear Him, and touch Him. They knew Jesus as a man, a human just like you and me. They were absolutely correct about Jesus humanity.

One of my more skeptical friends recently asked me a series of questions about Jesus leading to a logical conclusion. From the perspective of logic it does kind of make sense. The brief version of this conversation went something like this.

Friend: Could it be that God has died and we are still here?

Me: No, God is eternal and always exists. Always has, always will, God cannot die. (Romans 1:20)[1]

Friend: Was Jesus God?

Me: Yes, not only was Jesus God, Jesus IS God! (John 1:1-14)[2]

Friend: Did Jesus die for our sins?

Me: Yes, Jesus died for the sins of the whole world. (1 John 2:2)[3]

Friend: Well, if Jesus is God as you say, and God cannot die as you say, how did Jesus being God die for our sins?

My friend thought he had me there, and from logic he had a point. God can't die, but He died. Thinking about this makes me reflect on a Bible verse in Matthew. You see, when you're dealing with God, human logic isn't always going to get you the right answer.

125

> Matthew 22:29 Jesus answered and said unto them, Ye do err, not knowing the scriptures, nor the power of God.

In other words, we are about make a 'logic based' mistake because we are not taking into account the Scriptures that we established to be true, and the power of God that we cannot fully comprehend. Logical sense can only explain matters of logic. This is a matter of the supernatural God. We need to search the Scriptures to be able to answer my skeptical friend's final question about God dying.

In the previous chapter we established that Jesus said that He was God, and we can quickly read the Gospel accounts to see the many miracles of authentication Jesus performed. Jesus healed a man who was blind from birth[4], healed a man who had been sick for 38 years[5], and raised the dead[6]. Jesus has power over nature and humanity because He is God. But more important than healing the physical ailments of man, Jesus as God has the authority to forgive sin[7].

Jesus is unquestionably God based on all we've said so far, but what about Jesus the man? Again, we can quickly see from the reliable Scriptures that we have, Jesus was born like we are born. It is the Christmas story! Jesus had no biological father. He had a mother named Mary. The baby Jesus was conceived in her by the power of God, by the Holy

Spirit[8]. Mary had a 'normal' pregnancy from a physical standpoint except that she had never slept with a man. Even Joseph, whom she was promised to, had not slept with her. Mary was a virgin yet pregnant. It's not logical. But we need to remember that logic is not going to help us here. We need to know Scripture and the power of God.

After Jesus is born in Bethlehem there is very little childhood information about Him. In one chapter of the Bible we see something of Jesus boyhood life and we can learn something significant from the passage. Luke chapter 2 starts with Jesus birth and ends with Jesus as a 12 year old boy.

> Luke 2:41-52 Now His parents went to Jerusalem every year at the feast of the passover. And when he was twelve years old, they went up to Jerusalem after the custom of the feast. And when they had fulfilled the days, as they returned, the child Jesus tarried behind in Jerusalem; and Joseph and His mother knew not of it. But they, supposing Him to have been in the company, went a day's journey; and they sought Him among their kinsfolk and acquaintance. And when they found Him not, they turned back again to Jerusalem, seeking Him. And it came to pass, that after three days they found Him in the temple,

sitting in the midst of the doctors, both hearing them, and asking them questions. And all that heard Him were astonished at His understanding and answers. And when they saw Him, they were amazed: and His mother said unto him, Son, why hast thou thus dealt with us? behold, thy father and I have sought thee sorrowing. And He said unto them, How is it that ye sought me? wist ye not that I must be about my Father's business? And they understood not the saying which he spake unto them. And he went down with them, and came to Nazareth, and was subject unto them: but His mother kept all these sayings in her heart. And Jesus increased in wisdom and stature, and in favour with God and man.

Jesus, as a human had to grow and learn. Did you notice the last phrase? Jesus increased in wisdom and stature and in favor with God and man. We could say that we have one of those odd questions to answer again. How come God (now as a human in a 12 year old body) has to grow and learn? I thought God knew everything!

God does know everything. We call that omniscience. With that in mind, we also see that Jesus "increased in wisdom". Let's look at more scripture to get a handle on this problem we are facing.

> Philippians 2:5-8 Let this mind be in you, which was also in Christ Jesus: Who, being in the form of God, thought it not robbery to be equal with God: But made himself of no reputation, and took upon him the form of a servant, and was made in the likeness of men: And being found in fashion as a man, he humbled himself, and became obedient unto death, even the death of the cross.

See that phrase 'made himself of no reputation'. That is what's known as the Kenosis or emptying of Christ during His human life on earth. Kenosis is simply the Greek word for emptying. It is rendered here as the phrase "made Himself of no reputation". In referring to Christ in human form, Scripture speaks of the humbling of God to become man. Charles Ryrie gives us a definition; "In the Kenosis Christ emptied Himself of retaining and exploiting His status in the Godhead and took on humanity in order to die"[9]. The Kenosis is the explanation of how God, who cannot die, can die to save us from our sins.

I agree this can be difficult to understand. Don't feel bad, the most accomplished theologians in the world don't have a full explanation. I would like us to just stop and appreciate that for a moment. God is so great and complex that our smartest human minds cannot explain Him. Think about this too. If they could completely explain Him then what kind of God would He be? I am thankful for a great God that I can know personally even if I cannot completely understand Him!

We see that Jesus is God and man at the same time in the same place. Basically Jesus is two things at one time, but in Jesus case it is not a 50%-50% God-Man make up. Neither is it more heavily weighted one way or the other, as if we might say the God side is more important so it is 75% and the man side is only 25%. This is a case where Jesus is and always has been 100% God, and since His incarnation He is also 100% human.

That's hard to think about. Just remember that we cannot think or reason at the level that God does. There are things we don't completely understand.

> Isaiah 55:8 For my thoughts are not your thoughts, neither are your ways my ways, saith the LORD.

We cannot think His thoughts nor understand His ways. So it is obvious that we cannot completely understand Him. He has revealed enough to us that we can have a general understanding.

Here is an illustration that I hope will help us. Suppose the Wright Brothers, Orville and Wilbur,

130

are here with us. We are discussing aviation with a modern day fighter pilot. While the basic principles of flight are the same for the Wright Brothers and the fighter pilot, the whole idea of powered flight has changed. The Wright Brothers famous first powered flight was about 120 feet, or about 70 feet short of a modern day 747 wingspan. Wilbur was traveling about 10 feet a second while the fighter pilot can possibly go over 1200 feet per second. The Wright Brothers would have no idea how to interpret modern day flight because their thoughts would not be equivalent to the fighter pilot's thoughts. It is like that with God and man. We just cannot get on the same level and think His thoughts or understand Him.

Jesus, being completely God was made as a Human completely, but still being completely God. We don't have to understand it to believe it if we believe the one who is telling us! Our fighter pilot could explain modern day flight to Orville and Wilbur and they could believe it without knowing all the details, and we can know and believe God without total understanding. Admitting that we believe other things that we do not understand, just like Orville and Wilbur would, can help us as we deal with things we don't fully understand like the God/Man Jesus Christ. We can believe Him, trust Him, and even know Him without ever completely understanding Him.

Jesus as God and as Man came to this earth and lived a perfect life, never sinning in any way. Here is another thing that is hard to understand, a human who has never sinned. We all know a lot of people, we have people all around us and they are all sinners, ourselves included[10]. The Bible clearly tells us what we already know; all people are liars and cheats and more. We sin right from the start, and no one had to teach us how. However, our reliable Bible tells us that Jesus never sinned even though He was made as a man.

> 1 John 3:5 And ye know that He (Jesus) was manifested (was made in the likeness of men) to take away our sins; and in Him is no sin. (Parenthesis and underline mine)

Jesus never sinned! The reason that Jesus, who is fully God, had to be made in the likeness of man is to take away our sins. More specifically He became a man to pay the penalty of our sins for us. The cost for our sins is a steep one but not too steep for Jesus.

The Bible talks about the penalty of sins in terms of work. Most of us have had jobs in which we work in exchange for a favor of some sort, [I remember as a child picking up all the toys in the yard in exchange for a bowl of ice cream], but usually we work for money. Another term for the pay we get for doing our work is the word 'wage'.

Romans 6:23a For the wages of sin is death...

In other words the payment that we receive (wages) for the work that we do (sin) is death. That is pretty straight forward. Our works are not productive, but costly. So we don't get paid dollars or ice cream, we get paid death. Maybe a better way to say it is that because we have sinned we have to pay. The penalty of sin, death, is a debt that we owe. We have to understand death means separation. Think about it. When someone's physical body stops functioning, their soul (the immaterial part of them that gives them life, personality, and intellect) has been separated from their body, and the body no longer functions.

Sin certainly brings about physical death but the death we are really talking about here is the second death, separation from God forever in a place called Hell[11]. Hell is a terrible place and nobody needs to go there because Jesus, the God/Man stepped into the situation to make the payment, or take the payment/punishment if you will. The Bible uses the big word "propitiation" to describe what Jesus has done.

1 John 4:10 Herein is love, not that we loved God, but that he loved us, and sent his Son to be the propitiation for our sins.

Jesus propitiation for us is like a third party payment. We as sinners have a debt to pay for our sins. We have already said that debt or penalty/payment that is exacted of us is death. We are only humans and we cannot recover from death. So, in paying for our own sins we are cast forever into the lake of fire with no hope of recovery. Jesus, the God/Man, steps in and pays the debt we owe on our account and gives us His righteousness that He has on His account! So our account is paid and Jesus suffers in our place.

Jesus can do that from a unique perspective because He is 100% God and 100% man! As a sinless man Jesus died in our place for our sins! Jesus is the only one who ever lived that could do this for us! Read these verses carefully please.

> Hebrews 2:14-17 Forasmuch then as the children are partakers of flesh and blood, he also himself likewise took part of the same; that through death he might destroy him that had the power of death, that is, the devil; And deliver them who through fear of death were all their lifetime subject to bondage. For verily he took not on him the nature of angels; but he took on him the seed of Abraham. Wherefore in all things it behoved him to be made like unto his brethren, that he might be a merciful and

faithful high priest in things pertaining to God, to make reconciliation for the sins of the people.

Because we are flesh and blood (human) Jesus also became flesh and blood (human) so that He might destroy the bondage (debt). Jesus did not become and angel to cancel the debt for angels. He became a man to cancel the debt of humans. Jesus became like us to pay our debt; to make us free from it! Think about that for a while! Jesus the God/Man specifically came as a human to save humans!

Jesus needed to be a man to pay the debt of man. You may say, "But there is only one Jesus and there are billions of sinning humans." Remember though that Jesus is the God/Man. Jesus as a man could pay the penalty for a man, Jesus as the infinite God could pay the penalty for an infinite number of men and women. Now we can see clearly that the God/Man position of Jesus Christ enables Him to not only die for one man's sins but for an infinite number of mankind's sins!

There is one more thing I want to cover before I wrap up this chapter. Just because Jesus was in position to save doesn't mean he could sit back in Heaven and wait for the plan of salvation to "magically" work. Jesus had to actually do the work that would 'pay for the wage of sin'. Think about this. Babe Ruth hit the ball over the fence hundreds of times but he never scored the run until he ran around the bases, touching each one, then finally touching home plate. If Babe Ruth would miss second base, the opposing team could make an appeal and Babe Ruth's homer would not count.

God does not cut any corners does He? He did all the work needed to finish the job. It would have been much easier for God to do something else, but as He understands right and wrong, anything else would have been wrong. A short cut to eternity would have de-valued the whole opportunity! What Jesus did was so beyond spectacular that no one could even think of duplicating it, and so Jesus says...

> John 14:6 ...I am the way, the truth, and the life: no man cometh unto the Father, but by me.

And the writer of Acts speaks of Jesus and concurs...

> Acts 4:12 Neither is there salvation in any other: for there is none other name under heaven given among men, whereby we must be saved.

He can save us because He voluntarily sacrificed Himself for us. He fulfilled the requirements and prevailed, He is able!

Revelation 5:1-5 And I saw in the right hand of Him that sat on the throne a book written within and on the backside, sealed with seven seals. 2 And I saw a strong angel proclaiming with a loud voice, Who is worthy to open the book, and to loose the seals thereof? 3 And no man in heaven, nor in earth, neither under the earth, was able to open the book, neither to look thereon. 4 And I wept much, because no man was found worthy to open and to read the book, neither to look thereon. 5 And one of the elders saith unto me, Weep not: behold, the Lion of the tribe of Juda, the Root of David, hath prevailed to open the book, and to loose the seven seals thereof. (This is Jesus!)

Jesus prevailed! He was not only in position, He actually did the work!

Revelation 5:7-9 And He (Jesus) came and took the book out of the right hand of Him that sat upon the throne. (Because He did the work and paid the wage) 8 And when he had taken the book, the four beasts and four and twenty elders fell down before the Lamb, having every one of them harps, and golden vials full of odours, which are the prayers of saints. 9 And they sung a new song, (to Jesus), saying, <u>Thou art worthy to take the book</u>, (because You did the work) and to open the seals thereof: **for thou** (Jesus) **wast slain, and hast redeemed us to God by thy blood out of every kindred, and tongue, and people, and nation;** (He died and shed His blood for the people of the world!) (Underlines and parenthesis mine)

He is the only man ever able to die for someone else's sins. This is because He's not only a man, He is the God/Man! Jesus got into position to do this work, and He chose to fully do the necessary work to redeem mankind from their sins. You can sit and think about this for a long time and never fully comprehend it. He's worthy because he is in position and He did the work. He did the work and is in position because He is worthy. Nobody else could have even thought about saving mankind because nobody else is 100% God and 100% Man, in position to do the work, and loving enough to follow through completely. This is Who and what made salvation possible.

Jesus is worthy because of who He is and because of what He has done!

1. Romans 1:20

2. John 1:1-14

3. 1 John 2:2

4. John 9:1-11

5. John 5:1-9

6. John 11:1-45

7. Matthew 9:2-8

8. Matthew 1:18

9. Charles Caldwell Ryrie, Basic Theology, 1999, p301, Chicago Ill, Moody Publishers

10. Romans 3:23

11. Revelation 21:1-8

Chapter Eight

Take it!

Have you ever gone to the Mall at Christmas time and checked out the little kids as they go and sit on Santa's lap? There are little kids who count with their fingers each time they tell Santa each thing they want for Christmas. Others get close to him, get scared, and start running back to mom. (Then you see mom and the child up there with Santa, and Mom just outside the photographers frame.) Then there are the toddlers who will sit there on Santa's lap but not say anything. They just stare at Santa while he talks to them.

Once I saw a Santa who gave the kids a candy cane just before he let them down from his lap. Some kids would take the candy immediately, others were skeptical and slowly took the cane. Believe it or not, some of them were so scared of Santa that they wouldn't take the gift. I think to myself, "Hey Kid! He's handing you candy! Take it! It's free! Don't pass it up!" That is the way mankind is with God and the gift of salvation. It is almost too easy. Some won't take it. They think there is a catch.

Here is the thing. If God said that we had to do something in order to get into Heaven we would do it or die trying. Say for example that God said that every person who wanted to come to Heaven when they die must do ONE MILLION push-ups during their lives. What would you be doing instead of reading this book? PUSH-UP'S!!! All of us would be doing push-ups until we fell on our faces, and then we would rest and do it again.

Thinking about that for a minute. We would have to do about thirty six and a half pushups a day for seventy five years. Because no one does push ups as a baby or when they are sick, we would all be behind schedule from the start. We might not even hear about the plan until we are a teen, so realistically we would have to do many more each day to catch up. Some of us might even get ahead of schedule while we were twenty something so that when we age we could take it easier. We would try to meet the requirement wouldn't we?

So here we are, doing our push-ups faithfully until we get to the milestone of one million. One outcome would be that our men would be beefy strong, and then so would the women. Secondly we would be proud of what we have accomplished. WE did it! WE worked our way to Heaven! That would be the opposite of God's plan. The pride of working our way to Heaven would get in the way of our relationship with God.

Throughout Scripture God takes a dim view of pride. Here is just one telling example of how God feels about the proud.

> Proverbs 16:5 Every one that is proud in heart is an abomination to the LORD: though hand join in hand, he shall not be unpunished.

Every one that is proud in their heart is an abomination to the LORD! As a member of the human race we have all messed up on the scale of LARGE. By our self-pride we follow ungodly ways and not God's. Isaiah records the pride of the ungodly...

> Isaiah 14:13-14 For thou hast said in thine heart, I will ascend into heaven, I will exalt my throne above the stars of God: I will sit also upon the mount of the congregation, in the sides of the north: I will ascend above the heights of the clouds; I will be like the most High. (Underlines mine)

The ungodly one says "I will" five times here. He wants to take the place of God. Notice also in verse 13, "For thou hast said in thine heart". These were not just boastful statements by the ungodly example. This was the desire from within him. He was proud in his heart! When the desire of your heart is to supplant God or even just to compete with Him, you have the wrong attitude. The ungodly lose everything because of their prideful attitude, and the same would happen to us!

My guess is that after one million push-ups we would be very prideful and self-promoting just like Satan was at his fall. Our heart would be bragging about our accomplishment and likely even sticking it in God's face. "I saved myself!" "You made it tough but I'm tougher!" As I see it on the mission field and in my stateside ministry people want to work their way to heaven. God says it's not going to work that way because pride leads to sin.

Lucifer sinned from the heart and lost his position in Heaven. He pioneered worldly sinful thinking. Worldly thinking has three main components that very successfully turn mankind from God and Godly thinking.

> 1 John 2:15-16 Love not the world, neither the things that are in the world. If any man love the world, the love of the Father is not in him. 16 For all that is in the world, the lust of the flesh, and the lust of the eyes, and the pride of life, is not of the Father, but is of the world.

There we have it, the lust of the flesh, the lust of the eyes, and the pride of life, all three destroy God's purpose in the lives of people every day.

We don't have to go too far into the Bible to see the first recorded sin. It is in the beginning of the very first book of the Bible. Notice how all three phases of sin were involved in the very first transgression by man against God. They were instructed by God in Genesis 2:17 not to eat the fruit of that tree. Early in chapter three Satan planted a seed of doubt into the woman, Eve.

> Genesis 3:6 And when the woman saw that the tree was good for food, (lust of the flesh) and that it was pleasant to the eyes, (lust of the eyes) and a tree to be desired to make one wise, (pride of life) she took of the fruit thereof, and did eat, and gave also unto her husband with her; and he did eat. (Parenthesis mine)

Pride seems to come up over and over again causing sin. Simply because we are just discovering this pattern doesn't mean it is new. Pride has been a big problem from the very beginning. It is needless to say then that one million push-ups (and the pride that would come with them) would not be in the plan of God for salvation. We are speaking in fun about push-ups. Any work of righteousness performed in an effort to make our sinful selves acceptable to a holy God would produce deadly pride and would be counterproductive.

Our reliable Bible takes this issue head on and destroys the idea of salvation by righteous works. There are two main Bible passages I want to discuss here.

> Titus 3:5a Not by works of righteousness which we have done, but according to his mercy he saved us...

> Ephesians 2:8-9 For by grace are ye saved through faith; and that not of yourselves: it is the gift of God: 9 Not of works, lest any man should boast.

These verses are complementary to each other; in fact I want you to run them together as if they are one sentence. I hope we will see clearly that righteous works produce pride and they are not in the plan of Salvation. Here we go!

> Not by works of righteousness which we have done, but according to his mercy he saved us, for by grace are ye saved through faith; and that not of yourselves: it is the gift of God: Not of works, lest any man should boast.

It is by God's MERCY and not by our works of righteousness that He saves us. Mercy is defined as: God choosing not to give us what we deserve. Remember from the last chapter, the wages of sin is death? According to God's mercy He chooses not to give us death, and by His GRACE He chooses to give us what we do not deserve, eternal life. Because of God's Mercy we do not get what we do deserve, and because of God's Grace we do get what we don't deserve!

There is one more thing. It is not automatic. God does want us to respond to Him through FAITH. To restate it clearly, according to His Mercy and by His Grace He saves us through Faith, our faith in Him!

Notice how clearly our works of righteousness are denounced. Notice the opening phrase, "Not by works of righteousness", in the middle, "not of yourselves", and again at the end, "Not of works". At the very end we see the reason why works of righteousness do not work for God. It says, "Not of works, lest any man should boast". Prideful people boast don't they? Ungodliness was boasting when it said 'I will' five times in Isaiah 14 wasn't it? God wants no part of boastful pride because it is an abomination to Him.

Salvation is according to His Mercy, by His Grace, through Faith in Him. Did you notice my underlines? There is nothing there that is about us. It is all about Him, and God has planned it that way so none of us can boast or brag about our salvation. In fact it is not our salvation, it is His. We can't save ourselves, much less anybody else. Jesus was in position. On the cross He did the work for all of us, and He paid the wage of sin for us. It is His salvation!

Now there is one little phrase in the Titus/Ephesians passage that we have not discussed and that is just six words, 'it is the gift of God', speaking of salvation. It is a gift! Gifts are free, we don't work for them; we just receive them. Jesus paid for the gift of God with His blood and offered it to mankind. He traded His life to make a way for us to be free.

There is another thing about gifts. They are not yours until you take or receive them. It is just like the kids that were offered the candy cane from the mall Santa. The ones who took the candy had the candy to enjoy. All those who would not take the candy cane, whatever their reason, did not have one to enjoy. The Santa there had a gift for each boy and girl that came to him. Everyone was equal. Yet at the end of the day, some of the kids did not get the treat intended for them.

Our salvation is just like that. Jesus has the gift of eternal life for each and every human on the planet. He offers that gift to all equally. Some of us have taken that gift He offers by means of placing our faith or belief In the person and work of Jesus on the cross. Many of us don't have the gift of God because we've never taken it from Him, never trusted Him, never believed, and never put our faith fully and only in Him.

Many people in this mixed up world just don't know what to believe. Some might believe they can be good enough to get into Heaven, but the Bible says that we have all fallen short of the standard of God. God is holy. His standard is complete perfection. God views the individual as perfect when they put their faith in Jesus and their sins are covered over by His perfect sacrificial blood. Some believe in a system or organization to get them to Heaven. This thought is just like the push-ups, trying to work their way to Heaven. It won't work. Others have never thought about Jesus and the whole issue of Salvation or going to Heaven when they die.

Let's take a moment to think about salvation now while the ideas are fresh in our minds. There is nothing we can do to earn salvation so we need to depend on another Way. We have to face the Truth in order to find eternal Life. Here is what Jesus says...

> John 14:6 Jesus saith unto him, I am the way, the truth, and the life: no man cometh unto the Father, but by me. (Underlines mine)

Jesus is the only way to get to the Father and thereby to Heaven. He is the only true one who could qualify be a Savior, and because He rose to life eternal from the grave. Because Jesus died for our sins and conquered death in our place He can offer eternal life to us as a free gift. It really is that simple.

To those of you who are trusting in Jesus and Jesus alone to save you, my prayer and purposes for this book are simple. It is that you might be strengthened in your faith, and that you might be a strong and active witness for the Lord.

To those of you who have never taken the free gift of God's salvation my prayer and purposes for this book are equally as simple. It is that this book will shed more and more light on the subject of Jesus, who Jesus is, and what He has done for you. Furthermore my prayer is that you take (accept, receive) the gift of God (forgiveness of sin, a relationship with God here, and a home in Heaven someday) and make it your own by complete belief in Jesus.

To recap very simply, our reliable Bible says we are all sinners, and I believe we all know this is true. None of us can reach God's perfect standard.

Romans 3:23 For all have sinned, and come short of the glory of God.

The price we pay for our sin is a steep one, it is death. Separation from God in a horrible place called Hell FOREVER.

Romans 6:23 For the wages of sin is death...

God loves us and saw our need for a Savior. So He made a plan. He sent Jesus to die for us so that we could be saved through Him.

Romans 5:8-9 But God commendeth (showed) his love toward us, in that, while we were yet sinners, Christ died for us. Much more then, being now justified (Saved) by his blood, we shall be saved from wrath through him. (Parenthesis mine)

Because Jesus took up our cause and died, was buried, and rose again, only He can pay the wage for our sin. He owns the gift of God which is Salvation, and makes it available to us! That means all of us!

Romans 10:13 For whosoever shall call upon the name of the Lord shall be saved.

Notice that it says "call upon the name of the Lord". Call on Him or in my words, "take it". Take the free gift of salvation for yourself. Once you make the choice to completely and only believe in Jesus it is easy to ask Him for forgiveness of your sins, a relationship with Him, and a home in Heaven someday. The great news is that He will gladly give these things to anyone who will simply believe!

> Romans 10:9-10 That if thou shalt confess with thy mouth the Lord Jesus, and shalt believe in thine heart that God hath raised him from the dead, thou shalt be saved. 10 For with the heart man believeth unto righteousness; and with the mouth confession is made unto salvation.

Just say a prayer to the Lord. Simply direct your thoughts toward God and say something like this to Him. "Dear Lord Jesus, I know I'm a sinner, and I'm sorry for the bad things I do. I believe that you died for my sins and rose again from the grave to save me. I want to ask you, Jesus to forgive me and to be my Savior now, today. Thank you for the gift of salvation. Please take me to Heaven when I die. I ask this in your name, Amen."

Epilogue

What Happens Now?

I remember when my son signed up for indoor soccer as a child. He was young, maybe 6 or 7 years old. He didn't know much about soccer, but he was enthusiastic about playing. Mom and I liked it because it was indoors so we didn't freeze while we were watching the game!

The coach tried to get everybody in the game and into all the positions. Youth soccer is more about learning than winning. Our son asked to be the goalie and eventually the coach let him try. He knew he was supposed to try to prevent the other team from scoring, but he had no idea how to do it. He had no chance of defending the goal because once he got to be the goalie he had no idea what to do next!

Maybe you just trusted Jesus as your Savior, and you're happy about it, but you have no idea what to do now. Actually, you may have trusted Jesus for salvation before you read this book and simply haven't known what to do next for quite some time now. No problem. It is obvious that if no one ever tells you, you wouldn't know!

Here are some quick lessons on how to live the authentic Christian Life based on our reliable Bible.

First, you must grow spiritually. The Bible uses the analogy of a baby and its food supply.

> 1 Peter 2:2 As newborn babes, desire the sincere milk of the word, that ye may grow thereby:

We have all been a baby before. You don't remember your earliest months, but you have you been around another baby, right? Babies desire their milk, and they get loud if they can't have some when they want it. New babies have a single focus in life, themselves. If you run out of formula the baby starts crying because it is hungry. It doesn't stop when you say "let daddy go to the store, I'll be right back". The baby's desire is for that milk, and he or she does not stop letting you know until the baby gets what it wants. When the baby gets its milk it is nourished and physically grows bigger and stronger! We need to be like that with God's Word. We need to crave it, and study it so we can grow spiritually stronger day by day.

One way to accomplish this is to do a daily devotional with the Bible as your study book. I'm just talking about fifteen to twenty five minutes a day reading the Bible, praying, and applying what you've learned to your life. Like a baby constantly desires to be fed physically, we need to be constantly fed spiritually. There are many good devotional books out there to aid your Bible study. My favorite tool, the tool that I use to accomplish this in my life is the Word of Life Quiet Time Diary[1].

In the growth process we have to get involved with the ministry of the Lord to people. This includes maintaining a good testimony before our peers and using our gifts and abilities for God. There is a Biblical basis for this, and I don't want you to get confused, let me explain. Remember there is no work of righteousness that we can do to save ourselves? We used the example of one million push-ups. There is nothing we can do except trust and believe in Jesus and what He has done to save us. We used Ephesians 2:8-9 to show us that salvation is by Grace through Faith and not of our works so we cannot boast or brag.

What is true for obtaining salvation now looks different after we have taken the gift of God. Now that we are saved we are part of God's people and our goal is now to reach out to other people just like someone reached out to us with the message of Jesus saving grace. From Ephesians 2:8-9 just keep reading into verse ten...

> Ephesians 2:8-10 For by grace are ye saved through faith; and that not of yourselves: it is the gift of God: 9 Not of works, lest any man should boast. 10 For we (saved people) are His workmanship, created in Christ Jesus

> unto good works, which God hath before ordained (ordained or you can say 'prepared') that we should walk in them. (Parenthesis and underline mine)

We take in God's Word like a baby takes in milk and we grow. As we grow, we begin to live Godly lives and do Godly things to honor the Lord who saved us, and to reach out to others!

Then we need to help each other and support each other. We do this through fellowship and friendship within the local church.

> Hebrews 10:24-25 And let us consider one another to provoke unto love and to good works: 25 Not forsaking the assembling of ourselves together, as the manner of some is; but exhorting one another: and so much the more, as ye see the day approaching.

Find a good church that teaches the Bible. That is what is needed for growth. It is sad to say today that many so called churches are not focusing on our amazing Bible when they teach. These are the main things to look for: Are they teaching the Bible? Are they trying to reach others with the Gospel or truth of Jesus? Are most of the people at that church sincerely trying to live their lives according to the words of Scripture?

I know the word "study" doesn't appeal to most of us, but if you just learn one little thing each day and apply it to your life you will be a growing thriving Christian before you know it. There might be frustrations along the way. Find a tried and true Christian to help you. Many people get this help from someone older. A good mature friend that you can talk to will help you beyond what you can imagine. I know from experience that a mentoring relationship focused around Biblical teaching can be one of the most rewarding experiences of your life.

Finally, let me leave you with this encouragement from the Word of God.

> Philippians 4:8 Finally, brethren, whatsoever things are true, whatsoever things are honest, whatsoever things are just, whatsoever things are pure, whatsoever things are lovely, whatsoever things are of good report; if there be any virtue, and if there be any praise, think on these things.

May the Lord bless you!

1 Word of Life Quiet Time Diary is copy written by Word of Life International, Schroon Lake NY. www.wol.org